CW00970957

BUDDHISM 101

FROM KARMA TO THE **FOUR NOBLE TRUTHS,** YOUR GUIDE TO
UNDERSTANDING THE PRINCIPLES OF BUDDHISM

ARNIE KOZAK, PhD

Adams Media
New York   London   Toronto   Sydney   New Delhi

Adams Media
An Imprint of Simon & Schuster, Inc.
57 Littlefield Street
Avon, Massachusetts 02322

First Adams Media hardcover edition AUGUST 2017

ADAMS MEDIA and colophon are trademarks of Simon and Schuster.

For information about special discounts for bulk purchases, please contact Simon & Schuster Special Sales at 1-866-506-1949 or business@simonandschuster.com.

The Simon & Schuster Speakers Bureau can bring authors to your live event. For more information or to book an event contact the Simon & Schuster Speakers Bureau at 1-866-248-3049 or visit our website at www.simonspeakers.com.

Interior design by Michelle Kelly

Manufactured in the United States of America

10 9 8 7 6 5 4 3

Library of Congress Cataloging-in-Publication Data
Kozak, Arnie, author.
Buddhism 101 / Arnie Kozak, PhD.
Avon, Massachusetts: Adams Media, 2017.
Series: 101
Includes index.
LCCN 2017015053 (print) | LCCN 2017017217 (ebook) | ISBN 9781507204290 (hc) | ISBN 9781507204344 (ebook)
LCSH: Buddhism. | BISAC: RELIGION / Buddhism / General (see also PHILOSOPHY / Buddhist). | PHILOSOPHY / Buddhist. | RELIGION / General.
LCC BQ4012 (ebook) | LCC BQ4012 .K675 2017 (print) | DDC 294.3--dc23
LC record available at https://lccn.loc.gov/2017015053

ISBN 978-1-5072-0429-0
ISBN 978-1-5072-0434-4 (ebook)

Contains material adapted from the following title published by Adams Media, an Imprint of Simon & Schuster, Inc.: *The Everything® Buddhism Book, 2nd Edition* by Arnie Kozak, PhD, copyright © 2011, ISBN 978-1-4405-1028-1.

CONTENTS

INTRODUCTION

Buddhism, one of the world's five great religions, has upward of 500 million followers worldwide. The wisdom that Buddhism has accumulated in its 2,500 years of existence still transforms lives today, as it did in ancient India where it originated.

A contemporary translation of the beloved poetry volume, the *Dhammapada*, by Gil Fronsdal, starts with these words, "All experience is preceded by mind, led by mind, made by mind." This idea is at the heart of Buddhism. Buddhists practice mindfulness and compassion in all they do.

The Buddha was an Indian prince, Siddhartha Gotama. Although he lived in pampered luxury, he recognized that everything we see around us—including ourselves—will pass away. By prolonged meditation on this he realized that to achieve happiness we must put aside desire for the things of this world, both material and immaterial. Buddhism identifies the three most valuable things in life:

1. *Buddha*—everyone's potential for awakening
2. *Dharma*—the collection of the Buddha's teachings
3. *Sangha*—the community of practitioners

The path to freedom is realized by practicing the Noble Eightfold Path, eight disciplines (view, resolve, speech, action, livelihood, effort, mindfulness, and concentration) through which a practitioner can achieve cessation of suffering, a condition Buddhists call *nirvana*.

Buddhism 101 will introduce you to this religious tradition. You'll learn the basic principles of Buddhism and the various Buddhist traditions, ranging from Zen Buddhism in Japan to Tibetan Buddhism, practiced in temples high in the majestic Himalayas. You'll see that although there's a core set of beliefs common to all Buddhists, there is not a single Buddhism; instead, there are a wide variety of Buddhist beliefs and practices, depending on the country and tradition.

Today, Buddhism is spreading in the West and provides a way to look at many of the challenges that face society. You may already be familiar with—and even engage in—some Buddhist practices such as meditation and mindfulness without even realizing where these practices came from.

Whether you're interested in the origins of Buddhism, the nature of its practices, or if you want to find out how you can begin to live a mindful life filled with lovingkindness, *Buddhism 101* will answer your questions.

"Happiness," says the Dalai Lama, spiritual leader of Tibetan Buddhism, "is not something ready made. It comes from your own actions." In *Buddhism 101* you'll learn more about this way of looking at the world and discover how those who practice Buddhism create their own happiness and find inner peace.

WHAT IS BUDDHISM?

Religion or Philosophy?

Buddhism is one of the world's great religions. Behind Christianity, Islam, and Hinduism, it is the fourth most followed religion in the world. The question might be raised: Is Buddhism a religion at all?

RELIGION OR PHILOSOPHY?

Can you have a religion without god, a supreme being that created the world and intervenes in the lives of his (or her) creatures? It appears that Buddhism can be considered a nontheistic religion, according to Buddhist scholar Damien Keown, when it is considered along seven dimensions common to religion. These seven dimensions include:

1. Practical and Ritual
2. Experiential and Emotional
3. Narrative and Mythic
4. Doctrinal and Philosophical
5. Ethical and Legal
6. Social and Institutional
7. Material

Practical and Ritual

While the ritual elements of Buddhism may seem bare bones compared to the Catholic Church, for example, Buddhism certainly has rites and rituals that are public and private, many of which are associated with monastic life. Different Buddhist traditions place different emphasis on ritual.

Experiential and Emotional

The experiential dimension is the most important dimension of Buddhism. The Buddha was the exemplar. He transformed his life not through belief but through experiential practice. The heart of Buddhist practice is to be experienced rather than believed.

Narrative and Mythic

Buddhism is not without its myths and legends, including those surrounding the life of the Buddha, which can be read as a parable as well as a biographical account of the historical figure known as Siddhartha Gotama. There are many narrative elements in Buddhism, including the Jataka tales. Indeed, even the name "Siddhartha" is part of the mythology—an honorific title added centuries after his death.

Doctrinal and Philosophical

Professor Keown says of doctrine, "if by 'doctrine' we understand the systematic formulation of religious teachings in an intellectually coherent form," then Buddhism qualifies as having doctrine in this sense. For example, the Four Noble Truths are the foundation of the Buddha's teachings.

Ethical and Legal

Buddhism is widely regarded as one of the world's most ethical religions, having incorporated ethics into the foundation of the experiential practices. The central ethic is to "do no harm." Buddhism is predominately a path of peace. For example, the Dalai Lama has consistently advocated peaceful resistance to the Chinese occupation of his country, an occupation that has, by some estimates, claimed a million lives and destroyed 6,000 monasteries.

Social and Institutional

The *sangha* is the community of Buddhist practitioners, and it is one of humanity's oldest continuous institutions. Yet the sangha is not an institution in the sense that it has a central authority such as the Vatican. It is a diverse collection of people across nations and cultures that practice the Buddha's teachings in diverse ways. Buddhism is a socially engaged religion seeking to make positive changes in society.

Material

Buddhists have built breathtaking monasteries, caves, and carvings of the Buddha. King Ashoka left a legacy of stupas (dome-shaped structures) across India. Buddhist art is colorful and narrative. Buddhists make pilgrimages to holy sites such as the birth and death place of the Buddha and the places where he became enlightened and gave his first sermon.

As you can see, while Buddhism does not have a god and the Buddha is not regarded as a god, it fulfills the other criteria for a religion. You can adopt Buddhism as your religion or you can regard it as a set of experiential practices, such as meditation, that you can integrate with your own religious beliefs. Or, as many do, you can approach Buddhism in an entirely secular manner, as a philosophical system for living, eschewing all rituals, beliefs, and doctrine, just as the Buddha did 2,500 years ago in his search for a way to end suffering. You, just like the Buddha, have the same potential for awakening.

BUDDHA VERSUS BUDDHISM

Throughout this book a distinction will be made between the Buddha (the life and teachings of Siddhartha Gotama) and Buddhism (the religious institutions that have developed over the past 2,500 years in many different parts of the world). Not all Buddhism is Buddha, as these social organizations have migrated and developed over the centuries.

First Evidence

The first written evidence of the existence of Buddhism is found 130 years after the life of the Buddha. King Ashoka of the Mauryan empire of northern India made inscriptions containing references to Buddhism that date from about 269 to 232 B.C.E.

In the West, both the Buddha and Buddhism have been attractive and ever-growing forces for both personal growth and social change. You can embrace Buddha without embracing Buddhism. Buddha requires no beliefs, no affiliations, and therefore doesn't conflict with your own belief system whether you are devoutly religious or an atheist. Buddha's teachings are universal, transcending time and culture. If you have a mind, then Buddha is relevant to you.

THE AXIAL AGE

The Beginning of Spiritual Humanity

The Buddha lived and taught in the Axial Age, the period between c. 800 and 200 B.C.E. This period of humanity gave birth to the philosophies of Confucius, Lao Tzu, Zoroaster, Socrates, and Plato as well as the Hebrew prophets Ezekiel, Zechariah, and Jeremiah. And, of course, the Axial Age was the context in which the Buddha lived and made his mark on the world.

"A conviction that the world was awry [*dukkha*—filled with grief, pain, sorrow] was fundamental to the spirituality that emerged in the Axial countries. Those who took part in this transformation felt restless—just as Gotama [the Buddha] did. They were consumed by a sense of helplessness, were obsessed by their mortality and felt a profound terror of an alienation from the world."

—Karen Armstrong, *Buddha*

Advances in agriculture gave rise to food surpluses and the rise of cities bustling with commerce and political power. The Hindu world in which Gotoma was raised was one of ritual sacrifice. The Vedic worldview (adherence to the authoritative Veda Hindu texts) consisted of castes and believed that the entire universe was supported by sacrifices. The priest class of Brahmins was integral for the administration of these rituals. A strong belief in the afterlife and a soul that transcended death was part of the worldview Gotoma lived within. To get to the equivalent of heaven, one had to live a moral life and one's ancestors had to employ Brahmin priests to perform special rituals (*shraddha*). If one was immoral or one's family left you in the ritual lurch, your soul might dissolve.

Many concepts associated with Buddhism such as *karma* and *samsara* were imports from Brahmanism. The goal for Brahmanic mystics was to escape rebirth and samsara (the cycle of death and rebirth) by reuniting one's *atman,* or soul, with Brahman (the creator spirit). This union is the highest form of yoga. This final release is called *moksha.*

Famous Shramana

A contemporary of the Buddha was the *shramana* (ascetic social renunciate) Mahavira, founder of Jainism.

The Buddha transcended the received wisdom of Vedic India. He rejected the notion of an everlasting soul and made the radical observation that what is considered self is not a thing but a process, and a process that is ever changing. Suffering results not from living inside of a body (a belief that presumes a duality between body and mind) but from being attached to it. That is, suffering results from trying to hold on to a solid sense of self when everything is always changing, trying to cling to fleeting pleasures, and trying to push away unpleasant experiences. He succeeded in discovering a method that could bring an end to suffering, and this method can be reliably reproduced by anyone interested in trying. This method was not about achieving high or rarified states of consciousness but seeing the nature of reality clearly. That clear seeing is what leads to liberation.

BUDDHA, DHARMA, AND SANGHA

Role Model, Teachings, and Community

The Buddha pointed to 1) *buddha*—everyone's potential for awakening; 2) *dharma*; and 3) the *sangha*—the community of practitioners—as the most valuable things in life. In this case, buddha is not the person of the Buddha but the example that he set with his awakening.

Dharma has multiple meanings. In Buddhism, dharma is the collection of the Buddha's teachings. In the Buddha's time, wandering ascetics would meet each other and ask, "Whose dharma do you follow?" The Buddha was unique in that he did not follow another teacher's dharma but had figured things out for himself. Dharma also refers to the deeper truths that the Buddha's teachings point to. It refers to the truth of dukkha and the possibility of nirvana. Dharma is also translated as "natural law"—seeing clearly into the reality of things.

Equally important is the community, the sangha. The early sangha was comprised of the Buddha and his followers. This included his former five ascetic friends and the proliferation of people who followed, including poor farmers, wealthy merchants, and kings. People often joined the community after hearing one of the Buddha's discourses, which inspired in them a wish to end suffering. You could become a monastic or be part of the community as a lay practitioner.

Twenty-five hundred years later, these choices are still available and the sangha is one of humanity's oldest continuous institutions. Yet, it is not a formal community. It has no central authority, holds no annual conference, and has no membership roster. It is a loosely collected group of like-minded individuals who practice living the Four Noble Truths and other Buddhist teachings, practices, and rituals that have developed over the centuries.

"When we say, 'I take refuge in the Buddha,' we should also understand that 'the Buddha takes refuge in me,' because without the second part the first part is not complete. The Buddha needs us for awakening, understanding, and love to be real things and not just concepts. They must be real things that have real effects on life."

—Thich Nhat Hanh, *Being Peace*

Taking refuge in the Buddha does not mean that you are hidden and protected by a great and powerful force. It means to align yourself with the buddha and strive to become a buddha yourself. Similarly, you can take refuge with the dharma by aligning yourself with the teachings. Likewise, you can take refuge in the sangha. The sangha is not just about membership or social support. Of course, the sangha does provide support for your practice. To sit in meditation with a group provides a different experience. It gets you to sit up straighter and put more effort into your practice. And it also provides something intangible, something ineffable and powerful. The sangha is the glue that keeps everything together.

ONE DHARMA OR MANY?

Buddhism has proliferated in the world by changing and integrating other cultures and religions. As it moved from India eastward it was influenced by Taoism and Confucianism in China, by Shinto in Japan, and by Bön in Tibet. Buddhism arrived in the West in the nineteenth century. In many cases the traditions from the East have been imported and replicated here. But as Westerners practice and lead these communities, is a new form of Buddhism emerging? Is there a Western dharma? An American dharma? These are questions that the meditation teacher Joseph Goldstein poses in his book, *One Dharma*. What works to free Asians from suffering may not work for Westerners. At the same time, there is a risk that adapting the teachings to Western soil will dilute them or corrupt them into something else.

The basic teachings of the Buddha provide what is required for a nonsectarian form of Buddhist practice. It's all in the Four Noble Truths, and the core is overcoming suffering and dissatisfaction *(dukkha)* and living with mindfulness and compassion. All dharmas, that is, manifestations of Buddhism, share this in common: be mindful, be compassionate. The poet Jane Hirshfield's seven-word definition of Buddhism may also point toward one dharma, "Everything changes; everything is connected; pay attention."

THE BUDDHA

The First Jewel

The Buddha was both a human being and a symbol. When you take refuge in the Buddha you bow in respect to what he accomplished in his lifetime. When you take refuge in the Buddha you also bow to what he represents—your awakened nature. The Buddha's example can be a raft that carries you across the river of samsara. He can show you a path, but he cannot walk it for you. Once you cross over the river, you no longer need to carry the raft. In this way, Buddha is neither a god nor a saint but a role model.

Some people, especially those in traditional Buddhist cultures, may look to the Buddha as a source of salvation. In Tibet he is referred to as Lord Buddha. In the West, however, he is more the hero of an epic story of sacrifice and deliverance from greed, hatred, and delusion. He had everything, then nothing before finding the Middle Way. Through his voluminous teaching over a long career he has left a detailed path that any interested party can follow. He left a repertoire of methods that can lead to liberation. He was a great yogi and represents the potential for radical transformation, from a life of suffering to a life of liberation.

Lasting Legacy

The Buddha may have dwelled in obscurity, yet he decided to share his insights with those willing to listen. By doing so, he revolutionized humanity and the potential for transformation, compassion, and happiness.

Buddha-nature—the Buddha within everyone—is not created, but rather is revealed. It is present now, but perhaps obscured by your stories of desire and aversion. Buddha-nature is not made; it is not a destination. It is here right now. The Buddha showed humanity this potential.

Practicing the Buddhist path will help to make this buddha-nature accessible and clear. You will go through similar trials that the Buddha did if you commit yourself to these practices. This path is challenging, but anything worthwhile is. When you are struggling to keep yourself on the cushion, you can imagine the Buddha confronting the temptations of Mara, sitting steadfast and resolute. This image can inspire you to keep sitting.

Budai, Not Buddha

The fat and happy "Buddha" you've seen in Chinese restaurants is not Siddhartha Gotama, or Shakyamuni Buddha. He is Budai in China or Hotei in Japan. He is often depicted smiling and laughing. He is a folklore figure but is often mistaken for the historical Buddha.

The Buddha does not ask you to believe in him or to pray to him. Any peace of mind that comes to you comes from your own effort and not divine intervention. He shows you a path that you are free to take all on your own. There is no blind allegiance; there is only practice. See for yourself: you, too, can take refuge in the Buddha.

Living Buddha

Bearing in mind the Buddha's caution to avoid people who claim to be "enlightened," taking refuge in the Buddha can also mean finding an appropriate teacher. You might know of a Buddhist who is qualified to teach you the dharma in your community or at special dharma centers around the country. Find yourself a teacher who embodies the teachings of the Buddha. When you find a living Buddha—you witness the compassion and lovingkindness that is possible.

THE DHARMA

The Second Jewel

The second of the Three Jewels is the dharma. The dharma is the entire collection of Buddhist scripture and thought, including all modern Buddhist teachings, as well as the traditional, original teachings, such as the *sutras* in the Pali Canon. The dharma is all the spoken word and written text passed down through the generations.

Today there are many sources for the dharma: books, DVDs, MP3s, streaming Internet videos, and recorded dharma talks. There are also practice centers and monasteries. The proliferation of Buddhism in the West in conjunction with modern communication technologies has created an unprecedented availability of the dharma.

Nalanda University

According to Joseph Goldstein, Nalanda University flourished from the fifth to the twelfth centuries. "According to reports of travelers in those times, there were over two thousand teachers and more than ten thousand monks from all over the Buddhist world who practiced and studied there side by side. Today, although we are not all gathered on one campus, the ease of travel and communication has created a similar wealth of available teachings."

There are two types of dharma: that which can be read or heard—transmitted from person to person—and that which is realized. Realized dharma is dharma experienced through the practice of the Four Noble Truths—the realization of the truth, or awakening.

The dharma surrounds you. Any experience can awaken you to the dharma. Have you ever found yourself sitting outside, enjoying the wonders of a beautiful day? Suddenly you hear a bird call out, and its call is pure and sweet and fills you. You lose yourself completely in that moment, just listening to the sounds of the bird. The bird is the dharma; the bird teaches you something about awakening. In that moment, your story of "me" disappears and you awaken to a reality that takes over where stories stop. Anything can be the dharma: a bird, a work of art, a cup of coffee, a dog barking, the rain, even difficult experiences are dharma. Every experience holds the possibility of revealing some truth.

Venerable Master

Roshi is a title given to a Zen master, under whom a student must study if he or she hopes to reach enlightened mind. In Japanese it means "venerable master."

Zen master Suzuki Roshi tells us that it is difficult to keep our mind pure. In Japan, there is a phrase, *shoshin*, which means "beginner's mind." In Buddhism, the aspiration is always to keep this beginner's mind, this openness and readiness. Suzuki tells us, "In the beginner's mind there are many possibilities; in the expert's mind there are few." Do not take the dharma as an absolute, definable, and fixed reality. It changes just as everything changes. Be open to what you experience and avoid preconceived notions, especially those that apply to being on a spiritual path. As you journey on the path toward enlightened mind, let go of what you learn on the way and keep your mind fresh and clean.

THE SANGHA

The Third Jewel

Sangha is the community of Buddhist practitioners. The Buddha's first followers were his five former ascetic colleagues. Soon, though, he went from teaching men who were already renunciants to laypeople. A wealthy young man named Yashas became a follower and attained enlightenment under the Buddha's tutelage. Yashas's father also became a follower but as a lay practitioner (*upasaka*). Lay followers did not follow monastic rules but practiced the teaching by taking the Triple Refuge, or Triple Jewel: buddha, dharma, sangha. Yashas's mother also took refuge in the Triple Jewel and became the first female lay follower. In the days before Facebook, Buddha's teaching caught on through the social networking means available in the sixth century B.C.E. Friends of Yashas came, and friends of friends. Word spread. The Buddha sent the first sixty enlightened ones out to spread the teachings. Noted Buddhist scholar Kevin Trainor cites the Buddha saying, "Travel forth, monks, for the benefit of the many, for the happiness of the many, out of compassion for the world, for the well-being, benefit, and happiness of gods and humans."

Can the Average Person Attain Enlightenment?

Vacchagotta approached the Buddha and asked him if there were lay followers practicing the Buddha's principles who achieved "high spiritual states." The Buddha told Vacchagotta that yes, there were "not one or two, not a hundred or two hundred or five hundred but many more" who did.

Despite the Buddha's repudiation of the caste system, not everyone was welcome in the sangha. If you were a debtor, a criminal, or a runaway slave you may not have been welcome. The Buddha likely made such rules mindful of not offending his wealthy patrons upon whose generosity the sangha depended. In this way, he was a skilled politician and not detached from the practical realities of life. The sangha depended upon the patronage of kings and the wealthy. The most controversial issue where the Buddha did depart from social norms was allowing women to ordain as nuns (*bhikkunis*). It took some repeated pleading, however, from his aunt Prajapati.

The Buddha and the sangha wandered around much of what is today northern India. During the three-month monsoons, they would take refuge in special places built by wealthy patrons. They also did not want to travel during the rainy season for fear of injuring life that may be out during the rains, such as worms.

How Long Is a Meditation Retreat?

An auspicious-length meditation retreat is three months—the same amount of time as the monsoon rains when the monks *(bhikkus)* and nuns *(bhikkunis)* of the sangha sought refuge indoors. Since this duration is not practical for most people, ten-day retreats are popular.

Monastery (*vihara*) life consisted of meditation, initiation rituals, study, and recitation of what later became the Pali Canon. Two traditions emerged—the forest refuge where monks could do intensive meditation practice and the village monastery where they served the local community through education and rituals, and did their own practice. In some places, monks retreated to caves. Charismatic leaders led many of these communities.

CONTRACT WITH THE COMMUNITY

Lay practitioners were known as *upasakas* (males) and *upasikas* (females). A lay practitioner becomes so by formally reciting the Triple Refuge and committing to the Five Precepts in a ceremony with other members of the community. In some traditional Buddhist societies, for example, Sri Lanka, there is little emphasis on meditation and more emphasis on generosity (*dana*) and morality (*sila*).

The most basic act of dana is a food offering to wandering monks. Or, as in Sri Lanka, women will take prepared food to the monastery for the monks. In Tibet, generosity may take the form of the "tea offering," where money is donated so that all the monks can have yak butter tea. The laity can also "sponsor" the recitation of mantras or sutras. Money, clothing, flowers, and incense may also be given.

Generosity is an important part of spiritual practice. To give is to overcome ego-based attachment to things. It also helps to foster a sense of interconnectedness. According to the Jataka tales, which recount the "past lives" of the Buddha, the Buddha made a generous offering of himself to a hungry tigress so that she could sustain the strength to feed her young. Such selfless acts also generate merit (*punya*) for the lay practitioner, and the generation of merit is a primary motivation in Asian cultures.

On special occasions the lay community will adopt additional precepts such as not eating anything after lunch (only having lemon water), and not dancing, singing, listening to or playing music, ornamenting the body with perfumes, garlands, etc., or sleeping in high and luxurious beds (monks already partake of these restrictions). In Asia, the focus for the laity is on right conduct and right action, rather than on the meditative disciplines, and visiting holy pilgrimage sites. In Tibet, prostrations and turning prayer wheels are central practices for the lay practitioner.

"We take refuge in the Buddha because Buddha is our great teacher . . . We take refuge in the law, in the *Dharma*, because it is good medicine . . . We take refuge in the Buddha's community, or sangha, because it is composed of excellent friends. . . ."

—Dainin Katagiri

As you sit to do your meditation, perhaps you start wondering *why* you are sitting on a cushion when you could be watching *Law & Order*. Perhaps work beckons or the house needs cleaning. Without a sangha to keep you on track, the voices in your head that discourage you from your practice may get louder and louder until they crowd out that little voice inside yourself that urges you onward. The sangha can help bring you back to the path and hold you there. The sangha can be a powerful force of encouragement.

GENEROSITY

Dana ("donation") is a key Buddhist practice throughout the world. Giving generates a sense of generosity that is an antidote to the fire of greed. Giving also helps the practitioner to cultivate a sense of compassion for others and to overcome selfishness and the notion of an enduring self.

There would be no Buddhism today without the generosity of kings, merchants, and common people at the time of the Buddha and beyond. Giving results in merit, but the giving cannot be calculated solely to attain merit; giving should be done with selfless joy.

Some Buddhists believe that merit can also be transferred to others, such that your generous acts could be offered for the benefit of all humanity. In Tibet, for instance, family members of the deceased will offer merit to assist in a favorable rebirth. Even kings took this seriously. For example, Sri Lankan kings would keep "merit books" of all their good deeds and have these read back to them on their deathbeds to put their minds at ease.

According to Professor Trainor, King Sirisanghabodhi reflects the epitome of generosity. This fourth-century Sri Lankan king abdicated his throne when his treasurer mounted a coup against him. He became a wandering monk, much like Gotama did when he left the palace. Paranoid, the new king worried about Sirisanghabodhi's popularity and placed a bounty on his head. One day, a poor man shared his meal with Sirisanghabodhi and told him about the reward for his death. The king rejoiced upon hearing this news and asked the poor man to take his head as a payment for his generosity and to fulfill his own sense of perfection of generosity. After the poor man hesitated, Sirisanghabodhi cut off his own head!

UPAYA

Flexibility in Teaching

Upaya ("skillful means") refers to a teacher's ability to reach the student and admits a flexibility of approach to teaching Buddhist concepts. The Buddha reached people at all levels of awareness. He tailored his message to a person's experience, and he did so through the skillful use of stories, parables, and metaphors. Metaphors run through his teachings as a river runs through the countryside. Skillful means is the ability to make the dharma accessible. Modern-day examples of upaya would be teaching troubled teenagers mindfulness through music, as the meditation teacher Shinzen Young has done. Enlightenment on an iPod? Now that's upaya!

The Buddha's Metaphors

The Buddha used metaphors that included things familiar to the world of 2,500 years ago: oxcarts, fire, mountains, rain, streams, bows, and arrows. If the Buddha were teaching today, he would use metaphors from the technological present such as DVDs, email, and pause buttons on remote controls.

A TRADITIONAL METAPHOR

One traditional metaphor is the story of Kisa Gotami from the Buddha's time. Having lost her infant son to an illness, she desperately sought the Buddha for his reputed healing abilities. The Buddha listened to her plea and promised to bring her son back to life if she could bring him a mustard seed from a home that had never known death. She eagerly set out on her task but soon realized that death had touched everyone. She returned to the Buddha having "gotten" the concept of impermanence without him having to preach a word. Had he done so at the outset, this teaching would have likely fallen on deaf ears.

THE ORIGINAL METAPHOR

Enlightenment is a term closely associated with Buddhism. What happened to the Buddha under the Bodhi Tree is often characterized as enlightenment. This, of course, is a metaphor. When he overcame all the obstacles and temptations, the "lights" came on and he became "illuminated." Buddhist artwork often depicts Gotama with light radiating out in a circle around his head. But is this the best metaphor? The Buddha said he was *buddho* and that means "awake," not illuminated. The implications of each metaphor are different. Enlightenment makes it (enlightenment) sound like something heavenly and otherworldly. But awakening sounds like something you do every day, thus, making it more common and more accessible than you might think.

SIDDHARTHA GOTAMA

The Buddha

Buddhist texts contain few references to biographical events from the Buddha's life. However, historians agree that he did exist and lived a long and prosperous life—he died at eighty years old after teaching for forty-five years, traveling all over India to do so. Although the Buddha's teachings were preserved through oral recitation and first written down hundreds of years after his death, they are considered credible and accurate representations, for the most part. However, it is impossible to know for certain, and it appears that some material was added over the course of the centuries.

GOTAMA THE MAN

Little consensus can be found among scholars on the historical facts of the Buddha's life. This is due in part to the lack of biographical detail he shared in his teachings that later became the Pali Canon. A few key moments in the Buddha's story are known. Up until recently the year of the Buddha's death was taken to be either 483 or 486 B.C.E. However, new evidence suggests that it might have been as late as 400 B.C.E. His birth would have been eighty years prior to the earlier or later date (either 566 or 563 B.C.E. or as late as 480 B.C.E.). Many of the details of the Buddha's biography come from the poem *Buddhacharita* by Ashvogosa, which was written in the second century C.E.

Myth and Metaphor

The myth of the Buddha is colorful and strains our contemporary scientific view of reality. For example, Siddhartha Gotama was not the first Buddha nor will he be the last. The traditionalist Buddhist cosmology does not adhere to a linear sense of time, such that there have been an infinite number of Buddhas from the past and will be into the future. Taken literally such a view would violate the laws of physics that say time only moves in one direction—forward—and that the age of the universe is a finite amount of time. Fortunately, here and in every other place where myth meets metaphors, a literal belief in traditional ideas does not have to be held to derive benefit from the Buddha's teaching or from the example of his life.

Noble or Not?

While Siddhartha Gotama is often described as a prince and his parents Queen Mahamaya and King Suddhodhana, it is more likely that his parents were part of the nobility but not monarchs. His father was a magistrate of a smaller state in the Himalayan foothills. The elevation of the family to the highest royalty may be part of the mythology that has developed around the life of the Buddha.

As with the man himself, the life story of the Buddha can likewise be seen from different perspectives. Taken literally, it speaks of magic, wonder, and prophecy; viewed metaphorically it is a parable of sacrifice in the service of ultimate attainment. Certain elements of the narrative appear to provide drama to the story, but probably little in the way of historical fact. Siddhartha Gotama was born to a noble family in the Himalayan foothills, on the border of northern India and southern Nepal. His mother was Mahamaya, his father

Suddhodhana, and he was a blessing to the childless couple as they would now have a prince and an heir to rule over the Shakya clan, their small but prosperous region of the kingdom. The Buddha is popularly known as Siddhartha, which means "every wish fulfilled."

The Birth of the Buddha

Myth says that the Buddha's mother, Mahamaya, dreamed of a white elephant who entered her womb from the right side of her body. According to the legend, Mahamaya experienced a virtually pain-free delivery with the assistance of a tree that bent to offer its branches. The future Buddha exited the womb unbloodied and able to walk and talk. In some accounts, Gotama emerged from her right side, avoiding the "pollution" of the birth canal. The infant proclaimed, "I am the king of the world." His mother died a week later.

What Is a Brahmin?

The Brahmins were the priests, the highest class in the hereditary caste system of India. According to the caste system of Hinduism in ancient India, there were four classes of people: rulers and warriors (the Kshatriyas), business people and artisans (the Vaishyas), the Brahmins, and finally the unskilled laborers or untouchables (the Shudras).

It is generally agreed upon (with some variation) that when Siddhartha was but days old, his father, Suddhodhana, invited a large group of Brahmins to a feast at the palace so that they could tell the future of the newborn baby. Eight of the Brahmins concurred on the prediction that Siddhartha would either become a great and powerful ruler of all the land, or a great spiritual teacher.

They warned that if Siddhartha left the palace and saw what the real world was like he might have an existential crisis and turn toward a spiritual life. If he remained within the cloistered palace walls, he would become a great ruler of the world. One of these Brahmins, Kondanna, was convinced, however, that the young boy would become an enlightened one and warned of four signs that would influence the young Siddhartha and spur him to leave his home and commence a spiritual journey.

The Raising of the Would-Be King

Suddhodhana had no wish for his son to become a spiritual teacher, but longed for a son who would rule over the land. He decided to protect Siddhartha from the possibilities of a hard but spiritual path and vowed to keep him cloistered in the palace, lavishing riches and luxuries beyond imagination on the young boy.

YOUTH OF LUXURY AND PLEASURE

According to the legend, young Siddhartha was surrounded by beautiful things and kept captive within the palace grounds so he would not be subjected to the sicknesses and poverty of the people of the kingdom. He had everything he could ever want. His life was pleasure and luxury. He grew into a talented athlete, and an intelligent and charming young man.

One afternoon, when Siddhartha was eight years old, he sat under the shade of a rose apple tree watching the plowing of the fields as the town prepared for the new crop. He noticed that the plowing had upset the ground and that insects had been harmed in the process. The young boy felt sadness come over him as if he were attached to the insects. Yet the day was beautiful and the shade of the rose apple tree wonderfully cool. Joy rose inside him and he experienced a moment of meditative bliss. The compassion and love he felt for the insects took him outside himself and he was momentarily free, a foreshadowing of what was to come later in his life.

The Mother of Buddhism

Because his mother died, Siddhartha was subsequently raised by her sister, Prajapati. She is often called "the Mother of Buddhism" because she played a pivotal role in bringing women into the Buddha's circle. Eventully the Buddha allowed her to start an order of nuns, thus allowing women to enter in the realm of Buddhist practice.

When Siddhartha was sixteen he married his cousin, the beautiful Yasodhara. At age twenty-nine, his life was as much the life of luxury as it had been before, except his wife was pregnant with their first child. Indisposed and unable to entertain him, she beseeched her husband to find his own diversion. So Siddhartha wandered outside the gates of the kingdom.

THE FOUR SIGNS

When Siddhartha wandered outside he saw happiness, health, and good cheer everywhere he went. Then suddenly an old decrepit man with white hair, withered skin, and a staff to lean on crossed his path. Leaning over to his companion and servant, Chandaka, Siddhartha asked, "What is this?"

Chandaka explained that before them was an old man, and he told Siddhartha that everyone would age similarly one day. Siddhartha was saddened and shocked by the sight of the old man and wondered how he could continue to enjoy such sights as his garden when such suffering was to come later.

A second trip outside the palace grounds brought before the young prince the sight of a sick man with oozing sores. Chandaka had to tell him that sickness and pain befalls everyone. A third visit outside his sanctuary found him confronting a funeral procession and a corpse. Chandaka explained death to Siddhartha and told him it was inevitable for everyone.

The Sage

Buddha is also sometimes referred to as Shakyamuni, which means "Sage of the Shakya Clan," as he hailed from Shakya.

Finally, on another excursion with Chandaka, Siddhartha came upon a yogi in yellow robes with a shaven head and an empty bowl. Chandaka explained that this ascetic had renounced all worldly goods and gained peace by doing so. Siddhartha began to think this might be the thing for him. That night the opulence of the palace disturbed him deeply. The four signs had left their mark and the veil of luxury and riches had been removed. The world now seemed a place of suffering and pain.

GOING FORTH

After Yasodhara had borne Siddhartha a son, the cycle of birth and death seemed endless and oppressive to Siddhartha—life after life and death after death (or samsara: the endless cycle of becoming). Despite his love for his family and the birth of his new baby boy, he decided to "go forth" into the world the night he was born. Legend has it that he snuck out of the palace when everyone fell asleep, including, mysteriously, the palace guards.

His faithful companion Chandaka followed him out into the night but was soon sent back by Siddhartha to the palace. Siddhartha was now on his way, and once outside the palace grounds, he cut off his long beautiful hair, jettisoned his jewels and royal silks, and wore the assembled rags of a wandering holy man.

Another incident that propelled him forth happened at the palace after a night of partying with the beautiful consorts. He woke up in the middle of the night to see the beauties sleeping, mouths agape, drooling, and gnashing their teeth. In this moment, he recognized the impermanence of all things, especially beauty.

Truth or Parable?

The future Buddha's excursion outside the walls of the palace where he witnessed sickness, old age, and death for the first time, strains credulity. Even if his father tried to protect him from these things, family members and servants would have aged, died, and gotten sick at some point in Gotama's first twenty-nine years. This story is better viewed as a literary device to show his shock at the existential realities of life that motivated him to find a better way of living.

He vowed to live an unfettered existence. Family was not part of the life of a spiritual seeker; he had to go forth alone. He was motivated to find an end to suffering, by whatever means necessary, for the benefit of his family and for all of humanity.

Finding the Way

The forests in the kingdom of Kosala were fertile and green, and housed many seekers of truth called shramanas. Siddhartha became one of them. These ascetics were not seen as beggars and dropouts; to seek a holy life was a worthy cause. The young prince set out to find himself a teacher, and wandered far and wide over the Ganges plain, learning what he could from the available *gurus* (teachers). He spent time with two well-known gurus of the time, Alara Kalama and Udraka Ramaputra, and learned everything that these men had to teach.

Siddhartha was a meditation prodigy and quickly reached very high states of meditation (called *dhyanas* or *jhanas* in the Pali text). However, once he left the profound state of meditative absorption he found himself back in the realm of suffering. He had not gone beyond.

Siddhartha joined five ascetics and practiced the principles of asceticism to achieve enlightenment and discover liberation. Asceticism was believed to burn up negative karma and free one from samsara. It was the ascetics' belief that if they suffered enough in this life they could perhaps save themselves in the next. They sought to overcome the desires of the body through the power of the mind. Siddhartha practiced self-denial, mortification, meditation, and yogic exercises, searching for liberation from the ties of the material world. Siddhartha believed that if he could transcend the self he could free himself of the endless cycles of samsara and become enlightened—finally free from rebirth.

THE MIDDLE WAY

The Path to Enlightenment

Just as he had demonstrated himself to be a meditation prodigy, Siddhartha attempted to be an ascetic prodigy, only taking a grain of rice or drinking mud for sustenance each day. Together with his five companions he wore little or no clothing, slept out in the open no matter the weather, starved himself beyond measure, and even ingested his own waste matter. He lay on the most uncomfortable surfaces possible and inflicted severe deprivation on himself, convinced that external suffering would banish the internal suffering forever. He became very ill—his ribs showed through his skin, his hair fell out, and his skin became blotched and shrunken. But still he was plagued with desires and cravings. After seven long years of effort he was close to death.

"Moderate effort over a long time is important, no matter what you are trying to do. One brings failure on oneself by working extremely hard at the beginning, attempting to do too much, and then giving it all up after a short time."

—The Dalai Lama

Fortunately, a young girl named Sujata offered him some rice porridge and he took it, breaking his vows of asceticism. This was the beginning of his awakening and finding the middle path between the extremes of sensual indulgence and the dangerous denial of his physical needs. He recalled his meditation experience under the rose apple tree and realized there was another way to accomplish his goal. With the strength gained from that meal, the emaciated Siddhartha sat beneath a pipal tree and made a new vow: to not get up until he had found what he was looking for.

AWAKENING

As he nursed himself back to health, Siddhartha became very conscious of his movements in the world and paid close attention to how he reacted to his environment, watching his thoughts as they passed through his mind. He became aware of the movements he made while he ate, slept, and walked. Siddhartha slowly became mindful of his every gesture and thought. Mindfulness is the process of bringing attention to the present moment, away from thoughts of the future or the past, or judgments about the present. It's contacting the lived experience of now. Mindfulness made Siddhartha aware of every craving that passed through him and of how transitory these cravings were. Everything changed: Everything came and everything passed.

He noticed that all things were interrelated. The fruit was attached to the tree that was attached to the earth that received nutrients from the sky when it rained. The earth nourished the insects and animals, which ate the berries that came from the trees that came from the earth that were nourished by the sky. The animals died, the plants died, and so would Siddhartha. Life was filled with interconnectedness and change. All was impermanence. Everything that existed would die. He would die, his thoughts would die, his desires would die. The moment would die, and another would be born in its place.

Whether he worried about loss, loss was inevitable as change was inevitable. With change came fear. And with fear came dukkha. This word has no direct equivalent in English. It is most commonly translated as "suffering," like the kind of suffering that Siddhartha saw outside the palace—sickness, old age, and death. Dukkha also refers to something more thoroughgoing and can also be translated as "pervasive dissatisfaction" or a sense of things "being off center," "out of kilter," or "awry." Sometimes it is translated as "stress."

The Names of the Buddha

The Buddha is known by many names, including Siddhartha Gautama (in Pali his name his Siddhattha Gotoma), his birth and family name; Shakyamuni, sage of the Shakya clan; Buddha, the fully awakened one; and Tathagata, the thus-perfected one or the one who has found the truth.

ENLIGHTENMENT

As he sat under the pipal tree, meditating and watching his thoughts come and go, his mind started to break free of the constraints of his ego. He entered each moment fully present as his thoughts dropped away. This discovery under the pipal tree is usually described as enlightenment—his final illumination and transcendence of suffering. That moment has also been described as awakening.

Mara Gives His Best Shot

During his time under the tree, the Buddha's arch nemesis, Mara, appeared. Mara, who can be seen as a metaphor for desire, marshaled armies of beautiful women and alluring visions to distract

Siddhartha from his path. Undeterred, Siddhartha persisted with his meditation, transforming Mara's forces into flowers that rained petals down upon his head. Mara's final ploy was to show Siddhartha a vision of himself, the one called "Siddhartha." But this self, too, Siddhartha realized was not unchanging, not real, not worth clinging to. Striking a now famous pose, the soon-to-be Buddha reached down with his right hand to touch the earth as witness to his awakening—to his seeing through the illusions provided by Mara. Mara, having used all the tricks in his bag, gave up.

"Only when faced with the activity of enemies can you learn real inner strength. From this viewpoint, even enemies are teachers of inner strength, courage, and determination."

—The Dalai Lama

Siddhartha continued to meditate through the night and according to the scriptures first experienced all of his past lives, then the past lives of others, and then finally experienced what is known as dependent origination—the "causally conditioned nature of reality."

The Buddha

The legend says that after his time under the pipal tree (which became known as the Bohdi Tree, the Tree of Enlightenment), Siddhartha had changed. When he encountered other people, they could sense this change. Soon after the Buddha attained enlightenment, he walked by a man, a fellow traveler. The man was struck by the Buddha's unusual radiance and peaceful demeanor.

"My friend, what are you?" he asked the Buddha. "Are you a god?"

"No," answered the Buddha.

"Are you some kind of magician?"

"No," the Buddha answered again.

"Are you a man?"

"No."

"Well, my friend, then what are you?"

The Buddha replied, "I am buddho [awake]."

The name stuck and Siddhartha became the Buddha. At first, he was ambivalent about his discovery and feared that people would not understand it. It took some time and deliberation for him to make the decision to commence his teaching career, a career that would last forty-five years. His first students were his old emaciated ascetic friends, and the first lesson he taught was the Four Noble Truths. This first sermon in the deer park at Isipatana is often referred to as the first turning of the Dharma Wheel.

THE FOUR NOBLE TRUTHS

The Heart of Buddhism

The Buddha often considered himself to be a physician more than the founder of a religion. As a doctor he offered medicine to heal the illness of the human condition. As a physician, he provided a diagnosis for the human condition (First Noble Truth), an etiology (cause for the condition; Second Noble Truth), prognosis (Third Noble Truth), and prescription for the treatment (Fourth Noble Truth). Dharma—the truth reflected in these teachings—is the medicine. The Four Noble Truths are all you need for awakening.

TEACHINGS AS VEHICLE, NOT DESTINATION

The Buddha offered a metaphor: His teachings were a raft to carry the seeker across the river of samsara (a word referring to the cyclical character of reality). Once to the other side he cautioned them to discard the raft. Truth had to be personal, and they should not keep carrying the raft on their back in case it might be useful again some day. The teachings carried on your back in this way are at risk for becoming dogma, and the Buddha wished to avoid that. Any truth must be experienced firsthand and not taken on the authority of a teacher, including himself.

FREEING FROM SUFFERING

The Buddha's teachings were a pathway to letting go of suffering, freeing oneself from pain. The Buddha taught the Middle Way. He knew that excessive pleasure (a life built on sensual delight) or excessive pain (such as the life of an ascetic) led to continual suffering and not to release from that suffering. In his first sermon at the deer park, the Buddha spoke of the Four Noble Truths and the path to nirvana. He presented his truths as a program of action and not just ideas to consider.

Avoid Blind Faith

The Buddha cautioned, "If you meet the Buddha on the road, kill him." Was he advocating violence? No, he was urging his followers not to follow teachers with blind faith, especially those who claimed to be enlightened.

At this first sermon, the light went on for Kondanna, one of the bhikkus (monks), and he experienced awakening as the Buddha spoke. He later said it was as if he knew all the time and couldn't understand why it suddenly was so apparent to him.

The Four Noble Truths are as follows:

1. The Truth of Dukkha.
2. The Truth of the Cause of Dukkha.
3. The Truth of the Cessation of Dukkha.
4. The Truth of the Path That Leads to the Cessation of Dukkha.

Back to the Buddha's medical practice: The sickness is dukkha, which infects every moment of existence. The cause of the dukkha is craving or desire. The prognosis is good; while much of suffering is self-inflicted there is a place beyond this mess, and that place is nirvana. The way to get to nirvana (the prescription) is by following the Noble Eightfold Path (listed in the Introduction). Following the Path is the way to healing and the recovery of sanity.

THE TRUTH OF DUKKHA

The First Noble Truth

In the Buddha's words, "What, O Monks, is the Noble Truth of Suffering? Birth is suffering, sickness is suffering, old age is suffering, death is suffering. Pain, grief, sorrow, lamentation, and despair are suffering. Association with what is unpleasant is suffering, disassociation from what is pleasant is suffering. Not to get what one wants is suffering."

Dukkha is most often translated as "suffering" and certainly it refers to suffering. The world that the Buddha lived in was a world that knew warfare, great poverty, and disease. Life expectancy was short and infant and child mortality was great. One cannot progress spiritually if the truth of this suffering and one's own mortality remains denied. By extension, the suffering of others cannot be denied either.

The Dalai Lama's Wisdom

In the movie *Kundun*, the young Dalai Lama is asked about the causes of suffering. He responds with his characteristic humor followed by earnest wisdom, "I need to squeeze this brain. First one understands that he causes much of his suffering needlessly. Second, he looks for the reasons for this in his own life. To look is to have confidence in one's own ability to end the suffering. Finally, a wish arises to find a path to peace. For all beings desire happiness. All wish to find their purer selves."

But dukkha goes beyond these obvious forms of suffering of aging, sickness, and death. It also refers to a pervasive dissatisfaction that colors every moment of life. The Buddha described this aspect of dukkha by the very choice of the term. "Du" of dukkha means "bad" and "ka" means "wheel." The Buddha invoked the metaphor of a "bad wheel" to capture the essence of dukkha. It is more than suffering. It describes an oxcart whose wheel is off its axle, biasing every movement of the cart; or a wheel that is broken and out of true, a wheel that is missing a chunk. That bumpy dissatisfaction or sense that things are not right captures the more important aspect of dukkha. Buddhism is notorious for its principle, "Life is suffering." But this is not accurate and paints a bleak picture. Life contains many delights alongside its difficult aspects. Nonetheless, nothing in life escapes dukkha because even the pleasures of life are fleeting; everything is impermanent. In addition, the notion of dukkha as pervasive dissatisfaction suggests that much unhappiness is self-inflicted. It comes from misapprehending the nature of reality and the self.

"This is the direct path for the purification of beings, for the surmounting of sorrow and lamentation, for the disappearance of pain and grief, for the attainment of the true way, for the realization of nirvana."

—Buddha, speaking about the Four Noble Truths and the importance of mindfulness

Think about it this way. If dukkha is self-inflicted, then there is a way out of this misery. And it is to this possibility that the remainder of the Four Noble Truths point.

THE THREE MARKS OF EXISTENCE

Dukkha is the first of the three marks of existence. Dukkha is descriptive; it's the diagnosis. The second two marks are the culprits; they are part of the disease. The culprit *anicca* is best translated as "impermanence." Things are constantly changing.

Sequestering

Do you need to sequester yourself away from the world—like a monk would—in order to realize enlightenment? The Buddha believed the Path was for everyone and no matter who you are you can realize nirvana. Sometimes the most challenging practice takes place in the outside world as you are forced to work harder when confronted with the many distractions of daily life. Enlightenment may be easier in a monastery, but is available anywhere.

Anatta is the next culprit, and while not difficult to translate it is difficult for the Western mind to grasp. Anatta means "no self" or "not self." Anatta suggests that what appears to be "me" is not something solid, enduring, or stable. Whatever this "me" is, it is also subject to anicca. "Me" is always changing from one moment to the next and only gives the appearance of solidity. According to many religions, there is an everlasting identity known as the soul. The soul outlives the body and the mind, and it continues after earthly life is over. The Buddha rejects the idea of an eternal soul. Whatever this self appears to be, it is not solid and is always changing.

Self is a process just like everything else. And furthermore, what you take to be yourself is a metaphor for identity in that this moment is based upon previous similar moments from the past or future similar moments from an anticipated future. This process of comparison gives rise to a solid self or an ego that is more like a thing than a process. In our earthly life, a lot of energy is invested into this ego self. It must be identified with and protected; self-esteem must be enhanced, and this is often done in obsessional ways.

THE THREE FIRES (POISONS)

The three fires are greed (craving, desire, thirst), hatred (aversion, aggression), and delusion (ignorance, confusion). These are also known as the three poisons. The unawakened mind is inextricably intertwined in these three poisons or fires. They arise out of misunderstanding the three marks of dukkha, anicca, and anatta, and in turn, greed, hatred, and delusion are the primary cause of dukkha.

Each of these concepts is intimately bound up with one another. It's very likely that your day is filled with a variety of desires and aversions—things you want and don't want. These can be material things, sensory things, or emotional experiences. It's also very likely that you will attribute a sense of permanence to something that is not permanent and fall into the trap of the enduring self or ego (at least once!).

The three fires are a ubiquitous threat, and the Buddha's teaching offers antidotes for each of the fires. For greed he suggests generosity (*dana*). For hatred he suggests loving friendliness (*metta*) and compassion (*karuna*). For delusion he suggests the possibility of wisdom (*prajna*) waking up to a more accurate experience of reality.

THE FIVE AGGREGATES

In order to understand the nature of the self, the Buddha broke down the individual into five groups, or five aggregates of attachment, in his second sermon at the deer park.

The five aggregates he named are as follows:

1. The aggregate of matter (eye, ear, nose, throat, hand, etc.).
2. The aggregate of feelings (pleasant, unpleasant, neutral).
3. The aggregate of perception.
4. The aggregate of volitions or mental formations.
5. The aggregate of consciousness (response).

Each aggregate is subject to change. Your body changes constantly. If you are older than forty years old you know this to be true. In fact, most cells of your body change every seven years, and every atom in your body changes over about once every year. Every atom! From a physical standpoint there is nothing in you today that was in you a year ago. So, who persists? Feelings and sensations change constantly as well. Your ideas change. For instance, maybe you used to believe in Santa Claus. Now you believe in credit cards and bank statements. Your volitions change as well—volitions can be thought of as your intentions or the choices you consciously make. It could be said that volitions are the basis for your actions.

Volitional action changes as well. What you intend to do today will influence what you do tomorrow. And finally, you have consciousness (or response), which also changes constantly. You hear something with your ear and become conscious of the sound with your mind. You decide to act on the sound you hear. Your responses continually change.

Since you cannot act on that which you do not experience (you do not act on a sound you do not hear), you'll find that the fifth aggregate, consciousness, depends on all the other aggregates for its existence. The action or response you make based on the intention you had, which is based on your perception of your senses from your body, is *solely* dependent on each of the preceding phenomena. This is the Buddha's teaching of *dependent origination*.

The person you call "me" is made up of these five aggregates and nothing more. These aggregates are constantly changing. Therefore, the person you call "me" constantly changes as well. There is no fixed "me" or "I." There is no permanent self, nothing to grab on to. The only way out of this endless cycle is to see that the perception of a fixed self is an illusion that you are attached to. Letting go of this attachment is to liberate yourself from suffering.

These five aggregates together comprise dukkha, or suffering. If you think of a river, you will notice that the river is constantly changing. You cannot see one part of the river and stop to examine it and find it as fixed. Just like the river, you are ever changing.

THE TRUTH OF THE CAUSE OF DUKKHA

The Second Noble Truth

In the Buddha's words, "This, O Monks, is the Truth of the arising of Suffering. It is this thirst (*tanha*) or craving which gives rise to rebirth, which is bound up with the passionate delight and which seeks fresh pleasure now here and now there in the form of (1) thirst for sensual pleasure, (2) thirst for existence, and (3) thirst for non-existence."

The Second Noble Truth can be summed up in one word: *desire*, and it is known as the truth of arising (of suffering). Desire is like an overflowing river carrying you away to samsara (the endless cycle of becoming).

The teaching of Buddha
is like a great cloud
which with a single kind of rain
waters all human flowers
so that each can bear its fruit.

—Lotus Sutra 5

In the Buddha's Fire Sermon, he warned, "Monks, everything is burning. And what is burning? Monks, the eye is burning, visual consciousness is burning, visible forms are burning … Burning with what? Burning with the fire of desire, the fire of aversion, the fire of delusion." In other words, the three fires. The warning goes through the five senses and concludes with an invitation toward detachment as a path to liberation. You suffer because you reach out for certain things, push other things away, and generally neglect to appreciate that everything is changing constantly (anicca). The Buddha's admonition should not be interpreted as a condemnation of the senses, but rather a call to examine your relationship to your senses. Are they pushing you around, leading you into trouble, becoming an excessive preoccupation? Here again, the call is to the Middle Way, neither indulging in nor avoiding sensory experiences.

THE SOURCE OF DESIRE

Desire comes from sensation, and sensation is caused by contact with something that gives rise to the sensation. The cycle of suffering and desire carry on infinitely. For instance, you feel a gnawing sense of lack (the sensation) and see an ad for a powerful new car (the contact that forces the sensation or in this case exaggerates the sensation) that you believe will change your life forever. Your self-esteem, the ad, and the possible purchase of the car are causal, relational, and interdependent (the purchase is based on the sight of the ad that you saw when you were feeling bad about yourself). As you probably already know, such retail therapy does not lead to enduring happiness.

But the *most* direct cause of suffering is wanting something—desire. This desire is not limited to material objects, though they can certainly cause much suffering. It also extends to a wanting a serene disposition, your candidate of choice in office, a healthy life, a well-behaved dog, and attachment to ideals, ideas, and opinions.

CLOUDING THE TRUTH

The desire that you have for so many things keeps you from seeing things as they are. Everyone is addicted to some degree to thoughts of "me" and "mine." All this craving leads to pain. Have you ever felt a sense of lack and tried to fill it with things and experiences? Has it helped? Probably not. This is the truth of the arising of suffering. Desire keeps you trapped going nowhere.

THE TRUTH OF THE CESSATION OF DUKKHA

The Third Noble Truth

The Buddha said, "This, O Monks, is the Truth of Cessation of Suffering (*nirodha*). It is the utter cessation of that craving (*tanha*), the withdrawal from it, the renouncing of it, the rejection of it, liberation from it, nonattachment to it." To reach that state described by the Buddha is to attain nirvana.

Nirvana literally means "cooling by blowing" or "blowing out." What blows out? Adherence to the three fires (*kleshas*): greed, hatred, and delusion. It's like putting that fire out that the Buddha spoke of in the Second Noble Truth. This is the prognosis. The misery can stop if life can be approached with wisdom (*prajna*) instead of desire. It's hard to get to this realization without some meditation. By doing so, you examine the moment-by-moment changing nature of experience. When you do this, you see into the three marks and are no longer fooled by them. These marks, again, are dukkha (suffering; pervasive dissatisfaction), anicca (impermanence), and anatta (no self).

According to Buddhist scholar Todd Lewis, nirvana can be understood as "an impersonal state that transcends individuality" and as "eternal, tranquil, pure, and deathless . . . and the only permanent reality in the cosmos." Nagarjuna, the second-century philosopher (and second-most influential person in the history of Buddhism after the Buddha) adds to the definitional mystique of nirvana when he said, "There is not the merest difference between *samsara* and *nirvana*." What he means by this is that nirvana is beyond all conditions, beyond all categories, and cannot be grasped by the conceptual mind. It goes beyond intellect and must be experienced for yourself to be understood.

The Buddha advocated the following Seven Factors of Awakening:

1. Mindfulness
2. Discernment (that is, knowing whether an action will be skillful or unskillful)
3. Persistence
4. Rapture
5. Serenity
6. Concentration
7. Equanimity

Advanced meditation provides the opportunity to burn up past karma or the conditionings that you have experienced. It is akin to untying knots that have accumulated in your mind over a lifetime of experiences. Each knot that is untied, each conditioning that is deconditioned, every bit of karma that is burned up, moves you closer to awakening. Taken to its ultimate realization you will reach *samyak-sambodhi*—perfect and complete enlightenment. Language begins to fail in its ability to capture this experience, so you'll have to sit down and experience it for yourself. "Bliss" is one of the words that approximates the experience.

THE TRUTH OF THE PATH THAT LEADS TO THE CESSATION OF DUKKHA

The Fourth Noble Truth

To get to nirvana, you must traverse the Noble Eightfold Path. This path can be divided into three sections: wisdom and insight (*prajna*; right view, right resolve); morality (*sila*; right speech, right action, right livelihood); and meditation (*samadhi*; right effort, right mindfulness, right concentration). This is an entirely self-sufficient path. No outside intercessor is required. Indeed, the gauntlet is thrown down for you to work out your own salvation.

Buddhism is religion in action rather than belief. It is also practical rather than intellectual, as is reflected in the metaphor the Buddha used of the man shot by an arrow. Humanity is like the man wounded by an arrow, and the arrow is dukkha. Intellectual pursuits over practical application would be akin to hesitating to withdraw the arrow before you find out what kind of wood it was made from, who shot the arrow, and at what angle the arrow entered your body. What matters most in that moment is getting medical help—the healing dharma found through meditation—not philosophical speculation.

The fifth-century Buddhist teacher Buddhoghosa calls morality and meditation the two "legs" upon which wisdom leading to liberation stand. Morality is the foundation for meditation, and meditation is the foundation for wisdom. Each builds on the other and you can't get to wisdom without the other two.

This is known as the Middle Way. It does not promote excessive sensual pleasure or excessive self-denial. It is a moderate path that avoids extremes.

"This, O Monks, is the Truth of the Path which leads to the cessation of suffering. It is this Noble Eightfold Path, which consists of (1) Right View, (2) Right Resolve, (3) Right Speech, (4) Right Action, (5) Right Livelihood, (6) Right Effort, (7) Right Mindfulness, (8) Right Meditation."

—The Truth of the Path (*Magga*)

The Middle Way, or the Noble Eightfold Path, is a plan of action for realizing nirvana and the roadmap for Buddhist living. There are three sections of the Path that contain the eight "right" or "wise" ways to be, and each section is a platform for the next in a continuous process. Each of the eight aspects supports and interacts with the others. As the name implies, they are folded into one another as a field manual for a meaningful spiritual life.

What is meant by the word *right*? The Buddha uses the word *right* in the way we would say something is appropriate. You could just as well substitute *wise* for *right*. If you look at the list that follows, you will see that the Buddha is not prescribing or proscribing specific actions, because appropriate action depends on context. Even the moral foundations are not commandments for behavior. Instead, these right or wise approaches stem from directly experiencing which actions lead to happiness and which actions lead to misery. The goal is to transcend dualistic notions of right and wrong. Remember, the Buddha said, "I preach suffering and the end of suffering."

THE PATH

Here is the Noble Eightfold Path:

1. Right View
2. Right Resolve
3. Right Speech
4. Right Action
5. Right Livelihood
6. Right Effort
7. Right Mindfulness
8. Right Concentration

The Three Divisions of the Path

The Noble Eightfold Path can be divided into three different categories. The Pali word for each category appears in parentheses. They are as follows:

1. Wisdom (prajna)
2. Morality (sila)
3. Meditation (samadhi)

All the steps in the Noble Eightfold Path fall into one of these categories. Wisdom is comprised of numbers one and two: right view and right resolve. Morality includes numbers three, four, and five: right speech, right action, and right livelihood. Meditation is made up of the final three steps (six, seven, and eight): right effort, mindfulness, and concentration. These may appear in different orders and in different descriptions. The order isn't critical because the process is not linear; each part of the Path interacts with every other part.

Wisdom, Morality, and Meditation

Wisdom is made of right view and right resolve, and these two can be considered the hardest practices to master on the Noble Eightfold Path. Wisdom is gained through the practical experiences and insights that you have as a direct result of meditation practice. It is not gained solely through intellect, reading texts, or through rituals.

Morality or ethical conduct is comprised of right speech, right action, and right livelihood. All three of these elements have as their core a spirit of lovingkindness and compassion. Morality in Buddhist practice comes from a compassionate heart and mind and is expressed through the things you say, the things you do, and the occupations you choose. Finally, meditation consists of your mental disciplines of right effort, right mindfulness, and right concentration.

Practicing

The eight steps are not meant to be done sequentially but are to be practiced all the time, simultaneously, each and every one. Every day is an opportunity to practice. The Middle Way is a program of action. You can picture these steps as spokes of a wheel. In order for this Dharma Wheel to turn, all the spokes must be in good working order. Once you have understood what each step means, and have undertaken an attempt to practice the steps in your daily life, the Dharma Wheel starts rolling and you are headed down the path toward a happier life.

RIGHT VIEW, RIGHT RESOLVE

The Wisdom Steps

Right view means to have a total comprehension of the Four Noble Truths. Right resolve means a detachment from hatred (and cruelty). These factors are unique to the Buddha's teachings. The culmination of these views, based on morality and meditation, is the experience of prajna (wisdom or insight into the ultimate reality of things).

The Buddhist scholar Todd Lewis puts it succinctly about prajna, "a faculty that enables one unfailingly to see reality clearly amid the constant flow of human experience." This kind of seeing is existential (aware of the finite limits on life) without becoming morbid. This insight shows you the preciousness of life and the pervasiveness of suffering, not only for yourself but also for everyone. This naturally leads to a feeling of compassion (karuna) for all beings, and a wish to help them arises.

"All experience is preceded by mind, led by mind, made by mind."

—The Buddha

Right view is the ability to experience things beyond conditioned experience. It removes the biasing filters of past experience and allows you to experience reality closer to the way it actually is. It requires letting go of preconceptions, judgments, and reactivity developed over a lifetime of habit. Meditation (and its constituents, right effort, mindfulness, and concentration) will help you to identify your preconceptions, judgments, and reactivity and to see how they are active in your experience.

Right view is understanding dukkha, the causes of dukkha, how to stop it, and how to engage in a lifestyle that will address it. The goal is to live life well by minimizing harm to yourself, others, and the world. The goal is to experience things as they are without adding any preconditions, biases, or distortions. It is to find a natural happiness that is always available but obscured from your gaze in the way the sun is always there but sometimes obscured by clouds. Being in the moment is practicing right view.

The Eight Hooks

In the *Pathamalokadhamma Sutta*, the Buddha said,

Among humans, these things, namely,
Gain, loss, status, disrepute, blame, praise, pleasure, and pain
Naturally are impermanent, uncertain, and liable to change,
The wise, ever mindful, understand these things,
And contemplate them as always shifting and changing
Thus, delightful things cannot oppress their minds,
They have no reaction to disagreeable things,
They have abandoned all liking and disliking (for worldly concerns).
Further, they know the path of nirvana, dust-free and without sorrow,
They have reached the other shore of existence and know this correctly.

The Buddha warns about the eight worldly things to avoid. These four pairs of opposites are reflected in the preceding sutra.

- Taking delight in money, materials possession; feeling distress when separated from these things
- Taking delight in praise and things that boost the ego; feeling distress when receiving criticism or disapproval
- Taking delight in maintaining a good reputation or personal image; feeling distress when image and reputation are diminished
- Taking delight when making contact with pleasurable things; feeling distress when making contact with unpleasurable things

These are eight hooks for the mind and are thusly eight attitudes that make you vulnerable to dukkha (suffering; pervasive dissatisfaction, and so forth). The Buddha is cautioning against basing your self-worth, happiness, and well-being on their occurrence.

All things mentioned here are either not in your direct control (that is, it is something someone else does to us) or they cannot be controlled because they are always changing (that is, the fundamental truth of impermanence). He is not saying don't enjoy things but he is saying that enjoyment might be a double-edged sword if not tempered by wisdom of impermanence. He is saying don't take yourself so seriously. He is saying don't invest so much energy into self-protection. Don't base your self-worth on what other people think of you. In fact, spend less time on figuring out your self-worth and more time on paying attention to your experience (and while you're at it, why not focus on helping others, or at least not doing harm to others).

"It is very interesting and important to note here that thoughts of selfless detachment, love, and nonviolence are grouped on the side of wisdom. This clearly shows that true wisdom is endowed with these noble qualities, and that all thought of selfish desire, ill-will, hatred, and violence are the result of a lack of wisdom . . ."

—Walpola Rahula

Gain, loss, status, disrepute, blame, praise, pleasure, and pain are eight hooks to avoid and they may beset you constantly. Inevitably you may succumb to them on a regular basis. Alternatively, each moment is an opportunity to recognize the hook and to disentangle yourself from its barbed grasp. Mindfulness practice helps you to disentangle. To be mindful is to see how you are hooked and allowing fear to overtake you.

RIGHT RESOLVE

Right resolve involves intentions. The spirit in which you approach everything—a spirit of kindness, compassion, and harmlessness to your fellow beings—is essential to right resolve. The goal is to move away from the ego-related concerns of "me" and "mine," toward a lifestyle of service where your motivations are not ego-driven but more selfless.

A NOBLE PROCESS

The Noble Eightfold Path is a process. Don't worry about getting it perfectly at every moment. Do not expect that you will automatically wake up one morning with a wonderful loving feeling toward everyone that you express through tireless works of selflessness. It took many years to become conditioned the way you are and it will take some time to make changes. The Path provides the methods to accomplish this.

One of the biggest illusions people maintain is the illusion of separation. That is, the "me" as being separate from "you" and not just people, everything. The traditional belief, now supported by quantum physics, is that there is an interconnection amongst everything. And what we experience as solid objects are mostly empty space.

If you know that everything is interconnected you will behave differently in the world. Not only is everything interconnected it is also in flux—constantly changing. Wisdom invites you to recognize this and to enjoy the ride. Reality is a process not a collection of things. The world, including your body, is a ceaseless dance of energy and matter, interdependent and impersonal. It only becomes personal through the process of attachment and identification through language—"me and mine." The process of the Four Noble Truths can give you a direct experience of this truth. When interdependence is experienced, compassion for others and the earth arises naturally.

RIGHT SPEECH, RIGHT ACTION, RIGHT LIVELIHOOD

The Morality Steps

These three disciplines relate to morality and ethical conduct, and have a spirit of lovingkindness and compassion at their core.

RIGHT SPEECH

Speech is a powerful force and can be used for good or for harm. To practice right speech, you must speak the truth and avoid unnecessary communications such as gossip. While you might not always be certain of the right thing to say, you probably know the *wrong* things to say. Here are some examples of speech you might want to avoid when practicing right speech:

- Lies
- Slander
- Cursing or abusive language
- Raising one's voice unnecessarily
- Harsh words
- Speaking too much (rattling on)
- Gossip
- Creating enmity

Think before you speak and try to restrain your tongue.

RIGHT ACTION

Right action can be understood through the directive: "Do no harm," at least not intentionally. Where do you draw line? Is eating animals causing harm? Is wearing animal products causing harm? In the time of the Buddha, monks would eat whatever was placed in their begging bowls unless it was intentionally killed for them. The Dalai Lama eats meat for medical reasons. Does eating plants cause harm? In the Mahayana schools there is more emphasis on vegetarianism to minimize the risk of harm. The Theravada monastic code does not prohibit the consumption of meat. Right action is similar to right speech. Your actions should be harmonious with your environment, leading to peace rather than ill will. Try to do nothing that will cause harm to others. Obviously harmful acts include the following:

- Stealing
- Taking of life, human and otherwise
- Destruction of person or property or peacefulness
- Overindulging

Right action includes sexual responsibility—no adultery or prostitution. It also includes abstaining from using alcohol and recreational drugs in harmful ways.

RIGHT LIVELIHOOD

Right livelihood means to avoid harm through your work in the world. The monks in the Buddha's time addressed this issue by taking vows of poverty. Monks then and now renounce material possessions, except for a robe, a begging bowl, and few other items. Just as with sensory perceptions of the body, the goal is not renunciation, but rather a lack of attachment. There is no prohibition against the accumulation of wealth or of having luxurious possessions. It all depends on the relationship you have to these things. In fact, in the traditional view, great wealth may be a sign of good karma. Whatever the status of your karma, material wealth provides an opportunity to help others through generosity.

"The Eightfold Path is thus a path of self-transformation: an intellectual, emotional, and moral restructuring in which a person is reoriented from selfish, limited objectives towards a horizon of possibilities and opportunities for fulfillment."

—Buddhist scholar Damien Keown

Right livelihood asks you to look at your choices for work and decide if what you are doing to put food on the table is causing harm to anyone or anything else. Even more than not doing harm, right livelihood goes a step further and encourages you to do work that is helpful to others. It requests that you live an honorable life.

In today's world right livelihood can cause some confusion. You want to occupy yourself with activities that promote harmlessness and peace and cause no injury to others. Is being a bartender practicing right livelihood? That is up to you. How does your vocation affect your meditation practice? Is it helping or hindering? Can you practice harmlessness and drill oil? Can you work with nuclear weapons and maintain serenity for yourself and others? Right livelihood asks that you examine your occupation. Can you spend your work time, energy, and effort practicing peacefulness and kindness in the world?

It also should be noted that the Buddha considered no war a just war. Therefore, a profession in the military would not be considered right livelihood. Acts of violence were clearly against the Buddha's teaching.

RIGHT EFFORT, RIGHT MINDFULNESS, RIGHT CONCENTRATION

The Meditation Steps

The next three disciplines are all mental disciplines and directly relate to meditation practices.

RIGHT EFFORT

All this practice takes quite a bit of effort, so now you need to make sure you are using the appropriate level of effort, somewhere in between the extremes of laziness and overdoing it. Right effort also means getting rid of improper attitudes and thoughts. When unproductive or unsavory thoughts arise you must expend the necessary level to return your attention to what is happening in the present moment.

Remember how the Buddha expended great effort to realize enlightenment. He sat through the armies of Mara and did not move until he had accomplished what he set out to accomplish. You can think of Buddha sitting serenely when you are feeling restless during meditation to renew your resolve. To benefit from the Buddha's teachings, effort must be expended. There are no shortcuts.

RIGHT MINDFULNESS

Right mindfulness requires a foundation of right concentration. While practicing mindfulness meditation (*vipassana*) you will have a direct experience of the three marks of existence. By paying attention to, for instance, the rising and falling of your breathing or the arising and fading away of sensations in the body, you will have a direct experience of impermanence (anicca). When you see how your mind engages with painful stories or identifies with themes of loss or deprivation, you have a direct experience of suffering (dukkha).

When you practice and the mind achieves concentration and stays with the moment-to-moment phenomenological energies of being alive you have a direct experience of no self (anatta)—who is it who is meditating? You have an experience of awareness without identification with me and mine. This meditation practice can help you to weaken the bonds of attachment that keep you in samsara and to simultaneously promote wisdom—clear seeing into the actual nature of things. Meditation provides a crucible to experience the chain of causality, or what the Buddha called dependent origination in action.

Right mindfulness has to do with living your life in the moment and being mindful of everything you do. When you eat, eat. When you wash the dishes, wash the dishes. When you read, read. When you are driving the car, pay attention to driving the car (what a concept!).

"Mindfulness is the substance of a Buddha. When you enter deeply into the present moment, you, too, become a living Buddha. You see the nature of reality, and this insight liberates you from suffering and confusion."

—Thich Nhat Hanh

Right mindfulness asks you to retrieve your attention from the future, especially if that future-oriented attention takes the form of worry. Right mindfulness asks you to retrieve your attention from the past, especially if that past-oriented attention takes the form of regret. Once retrieved, bring your attention back to the present moment.

The Buddha was practicing right mindfulness when he was observing his thoughts, his sensations, his bodily functions, and his mind. The key to mindfulness is not to judge the contents of your mental experience as good or bad, wanted or unwanted, right or wrong. Right mindfulness and right effort go hand in hand. Without right effort there wouldn't be mindfulness, since mindfulness takes an appropriate degree of effort. Without mindfulness, effort would futile.

When you are mindful of your thoughts and actions, ethical conduct becomes possible in everyday life. This also connects to wisdom as well. From your direct experience you will start to notice which actions are skillful and lead to happiness and which actions are unskillful and lead to misery. This process is empirical; that is, you can test it out in real time, moment by moment.

RIGHT CONCENTRATION

Progress along the Path requires meditation. The mind must be your ally and not your enemy. The Buddha did not invent meditation; such techniques were being practiced in his day and for thousands of years before his time (although the method of mindfulness meditation was the Buddha's invention). Under the tutelage of his ascetic teachers he attained profound states of samadhi (concentration).

These trancelike states, while quite profound, always left him back in samsara once he was done meditating. The other risk of this one-pointed intensive meditation is that it could become addictive, promoting subtle craving for more and more sublime experiences. In a sense these trance states provided an escape from reality, not liberation from it. While concentration is an important foundation for training the mind it was not the ultimate solution he was seeking. The Noble Eightfold Path includes, in addition to right concentration, right mindfulness and right effort. Mindfulness was the method that most directly spoke to the impermanence of things and helped the Buddha to realize his awakening.

Right concentration is an important foundation for right mindfulness. It is by practicing the appropriate forms of concentration that you make mindfulness more available. One technique used in meditation for right concentration is concentration on the breath.

For example, you can pay attention to your breathing, noticing the sensations of the inhalation and the exhalation. If your attention is pulled away by thoughts, images, or emotions, you can bring your attention back to the sensations of breathing happening now. If your attention is pulled into the future or starts dragging the past along, you can disengage from those fantasies and memories and return attention to this sensation of the breath happening now.

This type of meditation is called one-pointed meditation, because you are focused on one point and keep coming back to that point. By practicing right concentration you can come to mindfulness of the moment. Right concentration supports right mindfulness. Together with right effort they form the third element of the Noble Eightfold Path, known as samadhi (meditation).

THE FIVE PRECEPTS

Guides to Ethical Living

The Buddha's teachings are at their core a prescription for ethical conduct in the world. By cultivating wisdom you minimize harm to yourself and the people around you and the planet. By embracing meditation, you find a path to find peace in the midst of everyday chaos and a world riddled with uncertainty. Ethical conduct is a foundation for meditation and wisdom, but this is not morality for the sake of morality or social control. You act in these ways because you know that it leads to greater happiness.

The moral precepts (sila) overlap to some extent with the Ten Commandments (don't lie, steal, or kill, etc.), and embody the Golden Rule (do unto others what you would have others do unto you). Translating *sila* as "morality" might create confusion; the term *ethics* might be a better choice. The basis for practice and the path to awakening are ethical precepts. They are done not out of some sense of moral purity but out of necessity.

The Five Precepts are:

- Do not destroy life.
- Do not steal.
- Do not commit sexual misconduct.
- Do not lie.
- Do not become intoxicated.

The fallout from unwholesome actions interferes with the mind's ability to train itself. In addition to the five silas, the Buddha also cautioned against another five unwholesome actions, making for a list of ten unwholesome actions. This list of ten actions to avoid can be grouped into things *not* to do with your body (don't kill, steal, harm with sexuality), speech (don't lie, don't be harsh with words, don't gossip, and don't engage in frivolous speech), and mind (don't get lost in desire, don't get lost in hatred, and don't get lost in wrong view).

In many Buddhist traditions, taking vows means to commit yourself to the practice of the five silas (not to kill, steal, lie, commit sexual misconduct, and become intoxicated). American Buddhist teacher Joseph Goldstein likens the ethical precepts to a warning sign on the beach, "Danger, Strong Undertow." The Buddha is the lifeguard who has put up this warning sign. The precepts are a template for living an awakened life.

DO NOT DESTROY LIFE

The First Precept

It's hard to kill someone in the morning and meditate with concentration and mindfulness in the afternoon.

Every living thing seeks its own survival and a version of its own happiness. This precept asks you to consider this in your actions. It's an invitation to revere life. Don't do things that cause harm to others. This is the practice of *ahimsa* ("not harming"). Don't kill, maim, or assault. Buddhists who believe in rebirth make the point that the being you harm may have been your mother in a previous lifetime. It also makes sense not to harm because the mind state that accompanies harming will be harmful to you as well.

Buddha-Nature

The Buddha taught that all sentient beings possess buddha-nature and are considered fundamentally good. Buddha-nature is the potential to awaken. Buddha believed that everyone has buddha-nature, no matter what they have done or how they look on the outside.

In regard to fellow humans the guidelines are fairly clear, but when it comes to the animal kingdom the considerations become more complex. Is it okay to kill a mosquito? What about one that may be carrying malaria? Can you protect yourself from a dangerous animal? What about insects and worms harmed in plowing fields? Remember Siddhartha's distress at seeing the plowed fields and the harm this caused its insect inhabitants? As with all the precepts, intention is essential. To deliberately harm is different than inadvertently harming, because it is accompanied by a different mind state and would, therefore, have different karmic consequences.

But it gets complicated. What if you hunt for deer? This is intentional taking of life to be sure, but in certain areas of the United States deer populations are so dense that many deer get killed on the highways, also causing damage to cars and people. So which action causes less harm? What about Native Americans, such as the Inuit, whose lifestyle is supported through reverentially hunting animals and using them for food, warmth, and tools? Are these people prevented from awakening? Surely not, and what you can conclude is that there are no "rules," and you should not be attached to rules (that's what really keeps you from awakening).

It would be impossible to go through life without harming another living thing, however hard you try. This precept invites you to take care with respect to life, letting kindness and compassion take the lead in your actions. It cautions against perpetuating the three fires through your actions, especially hatred, aggression, and violence.

To accomplish this you may have to be more thoughtful in how you conduct your life and consider how many animal products you encounter daily in your clothing, food, and other things. There may be relative levels of harm to consider such as eating beef raised on a factory farm living in huge herds, eating corn, and taking antibiotics versus one raised on a rolling hillside eating grass.

More dilemmas can be found in contemporary issues such as assisted suicide, abortion, and the death penalty. Here again, absolute rules cannot be formulated and you must use your self-knowledge and wisdom to discern appropriate action. Arguments can be made on either side of each issue and there is no central Buddhist authority, like the Vatican for Catholics, to issue policy.

DO NOT STEAL OR COMMIT SEXUAL MISCONDUCT

The Second and Third Precepts

The precept concerning stealing does not include just stealing tangible objects, but intangibles as well, such as ideas or time. The precept invites you to develop a sense of generosity toward others and respect for others' property.

GENEROSITY

The things you have can reinforce the illusory sense of a solid self, bringing considerations of "me" and "mine" into the mind. This is clearly the case when things are taken that are not freely given, but also the case when there is a lack of generosity. A lack of generosity reinforces the illusory sense of separation from others. This precept also points to the fire of greed. Greed could motivate you to take what is not yours. But it's not just stealing that is considered here. It's having more than your fair share. Westerners are privileged relative to much of the rest of the world, and even here in the West, some are more privileged than others. Many children in the United States don't get enough to eat, and yet dining at all-you-can-eat buffets is a popular and inexpensive form of entertainment whose sole purpose is to nurture the fire of greed.

You may have seen a bumper sticker that reads, "Live simply so that others can simply live." Here again is a reminder to walk the middle path between the extremes of indulgence and deprivation.

This is not an invitation to give away all your possessions. Rather, it is an invitation to consider the impact of your actions in the material world and how they affect yourself and others. The Middle Way is compatible with financial security. After all, the Buddha had to ensure the material needs of the sangha and did so by garnering the support of kings and laypersons who provided parks, temples, food, and other material support for those dedicated to the Noble Eightfold Path.

Money and Resources

According to The World Bank, the richest 16 percent of the world's population consume 80 percent of its resources. The poorest 20 percent consume 1.5 percent. Wealthy industrialized nations spend billions on cosmetics, perfume, entertainment, drugs and alcohol, and military spending. This spending is far greater than what is spent on basic education, water, sanitation, health, and nutrition for those in need around the world.

DO NOT COMMIT SEXUAL MISCONDUCT

Sex is a powerful force for creation, and it is a force for great harm when abused. Spiritual communities are not immune from sexual misconduct, as the scandals within the Catholic Church have shown. Even Buddhist communities have succumbed to sexual improprieties. This precept invites you to consider the power of sexuality and to use it mindfully with respect and responsibility for yourself and others. This precept is certainly a caution to avoid the obvious forms of sexual misconduct, and often refers to adultery just as the Ten

Commandments do. However, it is broader in that it reminds you not to do anything that can use the powerful force of sexuality in a way that harms.

Despite its puritanical origins, the United States is a highly sexualized culture. Sex is everywhere: in advertising, on television, in videos, and in movies. Pornography is a multibillion-dollar industry. Sex addiction is a growing clinical problem. Sex is everywhere and, like Buddha confronting the temptations of Mara, you will be challenged to be mindful in this arena daily. Sex taps directly into the fire of desire. If you seek lasting fulfillment from a transitory phenomenon like sex, you are bound to experience frustration. The Buddha taught that lasting happiness couldn't be found by pursuing desire in relentless fashion.

As with all aspects of the Middle Way, this precept is not an admonition toward prudery or even modesty. As with all the precepts it is an invitation to be awake around sexuality, an area that is challenging to be awake in because it is a deeply rooted biological drive compounded by media-based cultural conditionings. This precept is also an invitation to foster selfless loving in your intimate relationships along with harmony, safety, and enjoyment.

DO NOT LIE OR BECOME INTOXICATED

The Fourth and Fifth Precepts

The Buddha likened the tongue to an axe. Words can harm others; words can harm you, even your own words toward yourself. The fourth precept includes the four unwholesome actions of lying, speaking harshly, gossiping, and being frivolous.

This precept is much like the right speech of the Noble Eightfold Path. Do not lie, slander, be dishonest in any way, speak with insincerity, promote falsehood, misrepresent information, or gossip maliciously. Do not be indifferent to the truth in any situation or with any event that arises. Be truthful in everything you do and bring love and kindness into your environment.

Five Courses of Speech

The Buddha told his followers about the five courses of speech. Speech may be "timely or untimely, true or untrue, gentle or harsh, connected with good or with harm, or spoken with a mind of lovingkindness or with a mind of inner hate."

Words are powerful, and the invitation here is to be mindful and intentional about how you use your words. In addition to not lying, you are encouraged to avoid words (including your own private thoughts) that are harsh, critical, angry, or belligerent. The Buddha also encouraged his followers not to gossip because of the harm it can cause.

The final consideration for speech is to make your speech meaningful and to avoid engaging in frivolous or useless talk. The ability to speak is such a wonderful capacity, and it is one that can get taken for granted. If you remained silent instead of engaging in gossip and frivolous speech, how quiet would things get? The natural opening from these cautions is being receptive. When your mind is not entangled in lying, criticizing, gossiping, and wasting its time on frivolous talk you can enjoy a space for listening (and hopefully you'll be hearing the right speech from the person you are talking to!).

DO NOT BECOME INTOXICATED

This precept has a range of interpretations. On one end, there is strict prohibition against any intoxicating substance, even a single drink of alcohol. Some teachers include caffeine and tobacco as well. On the other end, the prohibition is against ingesting sufficient substances to induce intoxication and thereby impairment. In other words, it's hard to meditate with any skill if you are drunk.

There is a tradition to drink sake to celebrate the New Year in Zen temples in Japan. As with all the precepts, your approach can be empirical—based on your own experience—rather than following *rules*. You will find that being mindful of what you put into your body will support your progress along the path. The Buddha cautioned, "do everything in moderation, including moderation." That is, don't become attached to rules for the sake of having rules. This is just another attachment, another prison to encumber your freedom.

Media, food, and entertainment may be other forms of "intoxication." This precept is a caution to be mindful of all forms of consumption and to see if they contribute to suffering or if they provide you with a temporary release, only to cause a subsequent crash back into suffering. This precept brings the fire of greed into focus. Why do you consume? Can you consume mindfully? Do you have to consume so much?

The ethical precepts provide a foundation for mindful living that promote awakening, compassion, and wisdom. You obey the precepts not to be a "good girl" or a "good boy," but because you recognize the value in doing so. It is wise to act in these ways, and you'll know this from your direct experience. Acting without harming just makes sense and promotes your practice. It also makes the world around you a better place.

FIVE HINDRANCES TO SPIRITUAL PROGRESS

Obstacles on the Path to Enlightenment

The actions described in the Five Precepts can be seen as hindrances to practicing and living an awakened life. In addition to the Five Precepts and the ten unwholesome actions, the Buddha also discussed the Five Hindrances to spiritual progress.

The Five Hindrances are:

1. Doubt
2. Desire
3. Ill Will
4. Restlessness and Compunction
5. Sloth and Torpor

As you practice mindfulness and meditation you will become aware of each of the Five Hindrances arising in your mind. You will doubt that what you are doing is meaningful and worthwhile. Don't you have a million other better things to do? What is so important about just sitting here? All manner of desire, including sexual fantasies, will come up to distract from your object of meditation. You will deal with anger, hatred, and ill will as you dwell on the people and situations in your life. Restlessness and anxiety will arise, and you'll want to get off the meditation cushion. Sloth and torpor will make you sleepy and will make you want to watch television rather than examine your own mind.

OVERCOMING HINDRANCES

Each of these hindrances is something to work through. They can be looked at as gifts that further progress along the Path. Right effort is needed to counteract them. You must exert effort to cut through these resistances, just as the Buddha sat through Mara's assaults under the Bodhi Tree. Don't take them personally.

Khema

Ayya Khema, a noted Buddhist author of twenty-five books, became ordained as a Buddhist nun in Sri Lanka in 1979, when she was given the name of Khema, which means "safety." In 1987, she coordinated the first international conference of Buddhist nuns in the history of Buddhism, which resulted in the creation of the worldwide Buddhist women's organization, Sakyadhita. In New York City in 1987, she became the first Buddhist to ever address the United Nations.

It is important not to become entangled in the hindrances. Don't over identify with them. Everyone goes through them. See if you can observe these feelings and watch them arise and watch them pass. As Ayya Khema said in *When the Iron Eagle Flies*, "Cessation of suffering is not due to the fact that suffering stops. It is due to the fact that the one who suffers ceases to exist."

THE FOUR IMMEASURABLES

Limitless Abodes

Buddhism makes goodness an explicit virtue and aspiration. Goodness is embodied in what are known as the *Brahma Viharas* or the Limitless Abodes or the Four Immeasurables. These include lovingkindness or loving friendliness, compassion, sympathetic joy, and equanimity. Together they comprise what might be considered emotional intelligence.

The Buddha felt these qualities arose naturally when one realized the Four Noble Truths. These qualities are, in a sense, outcomes of living a Buddhist life. When you realize the causes of suffering and seek to overcome them, these qualities can come through. Each of them has at its core a lack of self-preoccupation. When you can give up your obsessive preoccupation with "I, me, and mine" a lot of energy is left over to devote to others in the form of lovingkindness, compassion, and rejoicing in their good fortunes. When there is no longer a self to protect, equanimity shows up in its place and you can confront any situation with an even and unperturbed mind. Each of these qualities has a "near enemy," a quality that seems like it but is not, and a "far enemy" that is its opposite.

LOVINGKINDNESS (METTA)

The Buddha said, "You can search through the entire universe for someone who is more deserving of your love and affection than you are yourself, and that person is not to be found anywhere. You yourself, as much as anybody in the entire universe, deserve your love and affection." In lovingkindness, you seek to generate feelings of safety, peace, well-being, and freedom for yourself, loved ones, strangers, and even your enemies. The near enemy to lovingkindness is an affection that is motivated by selfishness. The far enemy of lovingkindness is enmity.

COMPASSION (KARUNA)

Karuna is an ability to bear witness to suffering without fear. It is to be empathetic with a quality of openness, spaciousness, and stillness. Compassion requires the courage to see what is present and a willingness to hold it in your heart. It is a form of nonjudgmental care of yourself and others. When you are fully present with another you are in a compassionate posture. The near enemy of compassion is pity or sympathy. The far enemy of compassion is cruelty.

SYMPATHETIC JOY (MUDITA)

Mudita requires you to relinquish judgment and comparison, and to rejoice in the success and happiness of others, to appreciate the happiness of others. Mudita is an antidote to jealousy, envy, craving, and resentment, all of which are the far enemies of mudita. Mudita is nonselfish, nonattached optimism. Mudita balances karuna by preventing brooding; karuna balances mudita by avoiding sentimentality or ignorant optimism. The near enemy to mudita is exuberance, an excited state of mind that overlays a sense of attachment.

EQUANIMITY (UPPEKHA)

Upekkha is usually translated as "equanimity." This translation captures an important aspect of this state, which is a calm, tranquil mind in the face of any circumstance, even the most challenging ones. Upekkha can also be translated as "interest," and this interest is how you get to be tranquil during a painful situation. When you are interested in something you are paying more attention to it than to your own painful story about it. Equanimity brings a wise acceptance to every situation. Indifference is the near enemy of equanimity. It's not just dissociating from unpleasantness that gets you there, it's clear seeing. Being attached through craving and clinging is the far enemy of equanimity.

KARMA

The Nature of Responsibility

Karma is one of the fundamental concepts of Buddhism. A good grasp of the meaning and implications of karma will help you to appreciate the liberating potential of the Buddha's teachings. Karma is about responsibility—taking it and understanding how one thing affects another.

POPULAR MISCONCEPTIONS OF KARMA

Karma means "deed" or "action" in Sanskrit. However, action is not substituted for karma because karma carries much more weight than the simple understanding found in action. Karmic actions can be behaviors as well as thoughts and emotions.

Karma is one of the most popular and perhaps least understood concepts in Buddhism. There are multiple ways to consider karma. One way is "local" karma: actions in the present (including mental actions) that have an impact on future experiences. Another is "remote" karma: actions performed in this lifetime that have an impact on future rebirths. Remote karma, of course, depends on the idea of rebirth, which may be an alien idea to many people in the Western world. From a scientific perspective, there is no evidence for rebirth, and the Buddha emphasized local karma in his teachings because it was not necessary to invoke the idea of rebirth to understand the importance of karma. Your direct experience can reveal the working of local karma. What you think now will affect how you feel later. What you do now will bear fruit at some future point in time. This is different from universal balance, that is, "you reap what you sow," which is a common misconception of karma.

Here are some of the most common misconceptions about karma.

Misconception: Karma Is Retaliation from an Outside Force

How many times have you heard someone say, "She has bad karma," referring to someone who has had a run of bad luck. In the West, karma has often been interpreted as being equal to the principle of "an eye for an eye"—the retaliatory principle that you are punished with the same punishment you inflict on another. However, this is a misunderstanding of the Buddhist meaning of karma. According to the Buddha's teaching, you are not made to pay for past mistakes, nor are you rewarded for your past good deeds—rather you *are* what you *do* or intend to do. More to the point, karma is the process by which your actions shape your life.

Santideva

Santideva was an Indian Mahayana monk and scholar who studied at the renowned Nalanda University. He was born during the last half of the seventh century and was known for teaching the bodhisattva's way of life.

Since the Buddha did not acknowledge the presence of a theistic power, karma would not be associated with an external, objective judge. In the words of Santideva (a seventh- and eighth-century Buddhist teacher), "Suffering is a consequence of one's own action, not a retribution inflicted by an external power . . . We are the authors of our own destiny; and being the authors, we are ultimately...free..."

Misconception: Karma Involves All Actions

Karma only involves intentional actions. Therefore, if you were to step accidentally on a spider, you would not invoke karma. You unintentionally killed the spider but there was no intent to hurt the spider.

However, if you decide beforehand that you are going to kill the damn spider that is living in the garage and stomp on it with malice aforethought, you will experience the karmic ramification of an action that is laced with hatred and aversion. If you understand karma as one moment conditioning future moments, you can see the interdependent chain of cause and effect. When your mind is clouded by aggression this will generate particular effects. When your mind is occupied by peace this will generate its own particular effects. This effect will be on your own mind and will influence your behaviors that, in turn, will affect others.

"It is mental volition, O monks, that I call karma. Having willed, one acts through body, speech or mind."

—The Buddha

It might be helpful to set aside notions of "good" and "bad" karma because this distinction just creates confusion and reinforces misconceptions. Instead, think of skillful and unskillful actions. If you remember that actions include behavior and mental actions (thoughts, feelings, and images that you intentionally engage with and nurture), you will discover that certain actions lead to beneficial results; that is, you feel good and others around you feel good.

If you walk down the street smiling, you will feel good and others around you will feel good. This is acting skillfully ("good karma"). You will also discover that certain other actions lead to harmful results; that is, you feel bad and others around you feel bad. If you yell and criticize and kick the dog, you will be lost in feeling bad, later experience regret, and adversely impact those around you. This is acting unskillfully ("bad karma"). Acting from the three fires of greed, hatred, and delusion is unskillful; while acting from their opposites—generosity, kindness, and wisdom—is skillful.

KARMA AS THE ETHICAL CENTER

In Buddhism actions matter. And, therefore, karma serves as an ethical compass for your life. Karma is not a complicated concept. It is as simple as this: what you do, what you say, and what you feel will have an effect.

Effects of Actions

You can taste the effects of some types of karma right away; whereas other karmic actions will bear fruit at some point in the future. Karma points to the realization that everything is interconnected in some way.

But your actions have much greater effect than one day's span. Karma is a process of constant change. If you do skillful acts now, you can change your later karma. For Buddhists, the belief in karma is a guiding moral compass. However, do not worry or obsess on past actions. Take care of your life today. Live in the moment and change the present. Thereby you can change the future as well.

Traditionally, Buddhists would undertake their lives in a way to maximize their skillful karma by generating merit. They do this by donating food to begging Buddhist monks, donating money to the monastery, and doing good deeds. If you live your life in accordance with the Buddhist teachings and moral principles, you will automatically be on the way toward generating merit and limiting unskillful or destructive karma.

Whatever the ultimate truth of karma and rebirth, it can't hurt to live a good life that seeks to limit harming others and that seeks to be less selfish and more generous (in fact, research suggests generous people are happier). Another important consideration about karma is that not all suffering is the result of karma. Local conditions (for instance, a high temperature and internal conditions, such as a viral infection) have nothing to do with your karma. It is only through deep wisdom (prajna) that you would be able to know which bits of suffering are due to past karma and which are due to local conditions.

KARMA AND REBIRTH

In the traditional Buddhist view of the world, moving between lives and rebirths is not a random act but is determined by the actions in your current life. In this manner, you would be the heir to your own actions. As Peter Harvey says in *An Introduction to Buddhism*, if you commit acts of hatred—violent acts, such as murder, rape, incest, or bodily harm—you will be reborn into a life in hell. Here again the question arises whether this hell is meant literally or metaphorically. Unskillful or unwholesome actions of hatred and aggression leave one in a state that is very much like hell.

On the night of the Buddha's enlightenment he is said to have remembered 100,000 past lives. How is such a statement to be interpreted? How critical is a belief in rebirth to the early teachings of the Buddha? The cultural milieu of ancient India during the Buddha's time involved a vast and colorful universe of gods and goddesses. The Buddha speaks of gods and *devas* in his sermons, but he did not see them as godlike in the common idea of gods. These gods were trapped in samsara just as humans.

Rebirth is a fertile metaphor. It is not necessary to believe in rebirth to be a Western Buddhist or to derive benefit from the Buddha's teachings. On the one hand, as a metaphor, rebirth is a potent concept about the cycles of experience that occur right here and now. On the other hand, Tibetan Buddhists take the concept of rebirth literally and base much of their culture, beliefs, and rituals on this possibility.

Book of the Dead

The Tibetan Book of the Dead is a classic of Buddhist wisdom on the process of dying. It colorfully portrays the Buddhist cosmos and what to expect in death and rebirth and how to influence this process. It has become an influential text in the Western world for helping people to cope with death and dying.

Whether metaphorical or actual, "rebirth" occurs in every moment during *this* lifetime. When you breathe, your breath goes through a cycle of birth and death. As you move through life, you go through cycles of thought and emotion; everything is constantly changing. This is the cycle of becoming, and when characterized by greed, hatred, and delusion leads to never-ending cycles of suffering. The goal of Buddhist practice is to become liberated from these cycles of becoming that infiltrate every moment of life.

THE BUDDHIST CONCEPT OF REBIRTH

Like a Candle Flame

If there is no self and no soul, then you may be wondering: what is it that experienes rebirth? How can karmic fruits be carried into a next life? According to those who believe in rebirth, the personality of "me" and "mine" does not persist, but the mental energy, or *samskara*, is what Buddhists would say persists in the form of impersonal consciousness. That energy is what, for instance, the Tibetan Buddhists believe takes rebirth.

However, if human birth is considered to be precious and rare, you might be wondering what the universe was doing for billions of years before human beings evolved. The idea that human life is precious seems a bit humanocentric given the vast expanse of geological time where humanity is but a blink (unless this notion of linear time is dispensed). Again, the issue is whether you can derive benefit from the Buddha's teaching without having to take these ideas literally. The answer is a resounding yes.

How Long Is Buddhist Time?

The Buddha is said to have remembered ninety-one *kalpas* of time. A kalpa is an enormous amount of time. For example, if there was a mountain that reached many miles into the sky, and that mountain was made of pure granite, and once every one hundred years that mountain was stroked with a silk cloth held in the mouth of a bird, then a kalpa would be the time it took to wear the mountain away to nothing.

However, the notion of rebirth may be congenial to you. The Buddhist notion of rebirth is different than other concepts of reincarnation that you may be familiar with. Since there is no personal essence, "you" cannot take rebirth. Something carries forward but it is not your personality or "soul." You can think of it like a candle flame. One candle flame can light another candle. The flame "passes" to the next but has a unique identity. Within the system of birth and rebirth, there are many worlds and many ways in which one could be reborn—*endless* worlds and *endless* ways to be reborn.

Whether conceived of as actual rebirths or rebirth into the next moment, these cycles involve not only human births. A person is not necessarily born as a human in every lifetime. There are also animals, spirits, gods, titans, and the inhabitants of hell. The early Buddhists rejected the Hindu caste system, so in rebirth it was possible to move from a god to a human, an animal to a god. There was no safety in reaching a higher life form. Every life form was subject to death and therefore rebirth. Most Buddhists in the Western world would take these realms and forms to be metaphorical or mythical.

THE BUDDHIST COSMOS

The Three Realms

According to Buddhist cosmology, there are three realms—or types—of existence: the Realm of Desire, the Realm of Form, and the Realm of No-Form. These realms can be understood as the fruits of meditative experiences or the *jhanas* (the meditative states of right concentration). There are eight jhanas corresponding to the three realms. If you are in the Realm of Desire you have not yet reached the first meditative state. The Realm of Form corresponds to meditative states one to four, and the Realm of No-Form corresponds to the highest meditative states (five through eight).

The Realm of Desire includes the Wheel of Life and is a potent metaphor for karma, suffering, and the motivation to get beyond the three fires of greed, hatred, and delusion to the liberation of nirvana.

THE REALMS

Their Characteristics

Within the Realm of Desire are six categories into which you can be born in any given moment. These realms compose a circle; one is not "higher" than the other. These represent states, momentary and more permanent, that you may find yourself in any given moment. Each of the six realms depicted in this model can be understood as a state that you will experience at some point, perhaps many points, in your life. In the very center of the wheel, at the hub, are three animals representing the three fires (kleshas):

- Greed or desire is represented by the rooster
- Hatred or anger is represented by the snake
- Delusion or ignorance is represented by the pig

   The six realms are:

- The god realm
- The realm of jealous gods (titans)
- The animal realm
- The realm of hungry ghosts
- The hell realm
- The human realm

   Whether you end up as a god or a hungry ghost largely depends on your karma, your intentions, and actions. Nirvana is beyond these realms.

The Realm of Desire is named so because it is the realm in which beings perceive objects through their senses and experience desirability or undesirability. Desire is the root of suffering, and there is much suffering in the Realm of Desire. The Realms of Form and No-Form are not subject to the same experiences.

Bhadra Kalpa

According to John Snelling in *The Buddhist Handbook*, the most fortunate age to be born in is termed a *Bhadra Kalpa*. During a Bhadra Kalpa, at least 1,000 Buddhas will be born (over the course of 320,000,000 years). Each Buddha will discover the dharma and teach it for anywhere from 500 to 1,500 years, until a dark age sets in and the teaching is lost. Humanity is currently in a Bhadra Kalpa now.

The God Realm

According to Mark Epstein, a psychoanalyst and Buddhist practitioner, the god realm is "inhabited by beings with subtle bodies, not prone to illness, who delight in music and dance and exist in extended version of what has come to be called peak experiences, in which the participant dissolves into the experience of pleasure, merging with the beloved and temporarily eradicating the ego boundaries." In other words, this is a state that feels good but is temporary. There may be twenty-six "mansions" in the god realm, but there is a tendency to become complacent here. If life were pleasure and bliss, where would the motivation for transcendence come from? This realm also tends to be rather self-absorbed (no bodhisattvas here) and suffering persists, albeit in a subtle way.

Realm of Jealous Gods (Titans)

According to Dr. Epstein, the jealous gods, "represent the energy needed to overcome a frustration, change a situation, or make contact with a new experience." This is the realm of ego, mastery, and striving. The jealous gods can overtake your meditation practice in an ego-driven way, and this remains a pitfall. Striving cannot be overcome with striving. In other words, you can get caught in the trap of desiring more and more pleasurable meditation experiences. You may have had a taste of one of the jhanas and now your mind is fixated on having that experience again. Sometimes the jealous gods are portrayed as titans, or warrior demons (*asuras*), which have taken their human traits and used them in the pursuit of power. They are always in foul temper, always causing trouble for someone or other, and do not symbolize rest or peace.

Animal Realm

In the animal realm, you are caught up in desire and instinct, especially sexuality and the pleasures of the senses. It is a realm without awareness and states that are probably all too familiar to you. Animals are trapped in ignorance, and have no way of getting out of their instinct-driven behaviors. The animal realm is pure desire and tinged with the suffering that comes with desire.

"Never forget how swiftly this life will be over, like a flash of summer lightning or the wave of a hand. Now that you have the opportunity to practice dharma, do not waste a single moment on anything else."

—Dilgo Khyentse Rinpoche, scholar, poet, and a leader of Tibetan Buddhism

---

The traditional Buddhist view is that animals do not have sufficient awareness to generate good karma (due to the lack of conscious intentionality). "Does a dog have a buddha-nature?" is a question that divides Buddhists.

Realm of Hungry Ghosts

The fourth realm is restless spirits (*pretas*). Hungry ghosts are the most interesting form of preta. The hungry ghost has a pinhole mouth and a huge stomach and is therefore never satisfied. Adequate amounts of food can never pass through their small mouths and narrow necks, and when it does, immense pain is experienced. This is a metaphor for greed that takes the form of excessive desire.

Hell Realm

Fear, even to the point of paranoia, can characterize the hell realm. It's not the place you want to be. Early Buddhists, just like everyone else, had vivid imaginations when it came to suffering and torture. Metaphorically, you could be endlessly cut up, burned, frozen, eaten, beaten, or tortured in any number of ways, only to die and wake up and do it all over again. Some areas of hell contain abominable nightmares, unbearable sensory experiences, and horrible visions. The denizens of hell symbolize hatred, and the pervasive self-inflicted anxiety of dukkha. There are as many as ten hells in the Realm of Desire and the inhabitants must make their way through all of them to escape the anguish and suffering. There are realms where you may be hot (eight of those) or cold (also eight of those), or where you may be lacerated or eaten alive.

The third realm is the demon (asura) and is a state dominated by anger. In Asia, however, these demons may not be regarded metaphorically. Evil spirits can wreak havoc or cause mischief.

Human Realm

The human realm, on the other hand, is a very desirable realm to inhabit. It could be said to be the center of everything in the Buddhist cosmos. It is within the human realm that you have your only chance for enlightenment and escape from samsara. In any given moment you can be in any of the realms, depending upon your actions and intentions. One way to think about samsara is the endless cycling between these realms of experience. The human realm contains the seed of its own awakening.

Although humans still have some very negative traits, they are free from the extreme negativities of life as a hungry ghost, animal, or hell-being. Humans have the capacity to do right and wrong; it is therefore in the human realm that positive or negative actions are performed. This is a state where your karma gets played out. Buddhists who take rebirth literally see the human realm as the only realm that can influence their future rebirths.

THE REALM OF FORM

The Realm of Form (*rupa*) and its corresponding meditative states can be understood through the metaphor of the "higher gods." These meditative states correspond to contact with the form of the body and are the basis for vipassana meditation. They can also refer to forms of meditation that involve visualization.

The Realm of Form jhanas are:

- Rapture and pleasure born of seclusion
- Rapture and pleasure born of concentration
- Equanimity and mindfulness with pleasant abiding
- Equanimity and mindfulness, neither pleasure nor pain

The Buddha said, "Then quiet secluded from sensuality, secluded from unskillful mental quality, he enters and remains in the first jhana: rapture and pleasure born of seclusion, accompanied by directed thought and evaluation." The first jhana provides the foundation for the next. The Buddha said, "Rapture and pleasure born of concentration, unification of awareness free from directed thought and evaluation—internal assurance." The second jhana gives way to the third, "Then with the fading of rapture, he remains equanimous, mindful, and alert, and senses pleasure within the body. Equanimous and mindful, he has a pleasant abiding." He goes on to describe the fourth jhana, "Then with the abandoning of pleasure and pain, he enters and remains in purity of equanimity and mindfulness, neither pleasure nor pain. He sits permeating the body with a pure, bright awareness."

THE REALM OF NO-FORM

To reach into the highest jhanas is to reach the Realm of No-Form (*arupa*). Siddhartha attained the highest jhanas while meditating with his teachers Alara Kalama and Udraka Ramaputra. Once he came out of these rarified and sublime states he found himself right back into samsara. So even though these states are delightful, they do not represent liberation. Nirvana is not a state of meditation, but a release from all conditioned and constructed existence.

These meditative states are based on profound concentration. The Buddha described these states as "the complete transcending of perceptions of form, with the disappearance of perceptions of resistance." The practitioner will experience "infinite space" and will then transcend infinite space into "infinite consciousness." From infinite consciousness the practitioner will transcend into the "dimension of nothingness." This dimension of nothingness itself is transcended, and the practitioner will experience the dimension of "neither perception or non-perception." These states correspond to the jhanas five through eight.

The Realm of No-Form jhanas are:

- Infinite space
- Infinite consciousness
- Nothingness
- Neither perception nor non-perception

DEPENDENT ORIGINATION

The Causal Chain of Becoming

Dependent origination is the most original and radical of the Buddha's teachings. It describes the process that perpetuates the suffering and pervasive dissatisfaction of dukkha. Noah Levine provides an example of the process of dependent origination in his book *Against the Stream*. The twelve steps of the process include: (1) *ignorance* that leads to (2) *mental formations* (that is, thoughts, emotions, images) that lead to (3) *consciousness* that requires (4) *material form* (that is, something to be conscious of) that has (5) *six senses* (the basic five plus another sense of mind) that create stimuli that generate (6) *contact* that gives rise to sense impressions that generate (7) *feelings* (that are either pleasant, unpleasant, or neutral) that generate (8) *craving* (that seeks to either keep or push away the feeling) that leads to (9) *grasping* (or pushing away) that produces (10) *becoming* (which means to identify with the experience; to take it personally) that leads to (11) *birth* (taking form around the grasping) that leads to (12) *suffering* or pervasive dissatisfaction.

Consider an example. You are walking down the street on automatic pilot, lost in some story about the future or the past (ignorance). You see a bar and think to yourself, "I'd really enjoy a beer" (mental formation). You decide to go into the bar and plan to order a beer (consciousness). You walk into the bar. Inside the bar your senses contact a visual array of bottles at the bar, the smells, and the sounds (material form). You think of the touch of the bottle and the taste of the beer, and then you imagine which of the many beers you will order (six senses). The beers look good and you also notice the whiskey selection (contact). This contact gives rise to a pleasant feeling of expectation (feelings). You decide to order a boot-sized beer with a whiskey chaser (craving). You drink that one and then another despite knowing that you've probably had enough (grasping). You regret having drunk so much and wish you hadn't gone into the bar at all (becoming). You castigate yourself for your weakness; you call yourself a "loser" (birth). You feel sick to your stomach (suffering).

It's the process of karma in action. One mind moment leads to the next. Behavior, thoughts, and feelings all affect each other in a ceaseless process. And if you are not mindful, the process will lead to suffering. Being mindful gives you the opportunity to break the cycle of becoming, break out of samsara, and avoid suffering.

MAKING SENSE OF THE COSMOS

Whether the devas are to be considered real or metaphorical they provide a colorful element to Buddhism.

To contrast Buddhism in its more secularized form, consider this quote from Professor Kevin Trainor describing worship of the god Kataragama in Sri Lanka: "Worshippers seek the god's favor by engaging in various austere physical practices, including rolling in scorching sand, piercing their cheeks, tongue, and other body parts with skewers or hooks, and walking across burning coals." This type of worship that has emerged more recently might be explained by the growing population's need for immediate emotional gratification from a god-like figure, rather than "the ideals of sensual and emotional restraint that have traditionally characterized Sri Lankan Buddhism."

Nothing stays the same.

BODHISATTVAS

The Enlightened Ones

Much as the Theravada student strives to become an *arhat*—a spiritually enlightened individual—so the Mahayana student strives to become a bodhisattva. A bodhisattva is a person who has already attained enlightenment, or who is ready to attain enlightenment but puts off his or her own final enlightenment to reenter the cycle of samsara to save all sentient beings. A bodhisattva is the ultimate in compassion, and Mahayana Buddhists believe that enlightenment can be attained not only by striving individually but also by helping others to achieve enlightenment.

Every bodhisattva resolves to realize the Four Great Vows:

1. Sentient beings are numberless: I vow to save them.
2. Desires are inexhaustible: I vow to put an end to them.
3. The dharmas are boundless: I vow to master them.
4. The Buddha way is unattainable: I vow to attain it.

Bodhisattvas willingly seek to be reborn into the endless cycle of samsara so that they can constantly help others toward their own enlightened state. They need wisdom so that they can discern how to help others toward nirvana. Bodhisattvas employ compassion and love for all beings. They use upaya (skillful means) to accomplish their aim of benefitting all sentient beings.

Inherent within skillful means is wisdom—the ability to discern how to help each sentient being toward enlightenment. Wisdom heart is referred to as *bodhicitta*—the quality that allows them to be open to the suffering of others. Therefore, someone who desires to become a bodhisattva will develop and then generate bodhicitta. As you can see from the concept of the bodhisattva, Mahayana traditions rely more explicitly on concepts of rebirth, whether taken literally or metaphorically.

In addition to generating bodhicitta, the bodhisattva also strives for the Six Perfections. These Six Perfections are:

1. Concentration (meditation)
2. Giving
3. Morality
4. Patience
5. Persistence
6. Wisdom

Without the explicit commitment to rebirth for the benefit of all sentient beings, Mahayanists looked down upon Theravada practitioners and called them *shravakas* ("listeners"). According to them, being an arhat (an enlightened one) is not enough; one must strive to become a Buddha. Without that commitment, Theravada appears to honor the letter of practice versus the spirit of the practice—a wish to benefit everyone. If one does not believe in rebirth, this distinction becomes moot, but in the Buddha's day these were very much living arguments.

Since there haven't been any more Buddhas in the past 2,500 years, the argument likewise seems moot. A bodhisattva can also be understood as a future Buddha. If you take the bodhisattva vows, you undertake the arduous journey toward not just enlightenment but buddhahood. Good luck! The bodhisattva trucks in compassion and wisdom, and these virtues are more explicitly pursued and codified in the Mahayana traditions.

BUDDHISM AFTER BUDDHA

The Spread of the Sangha

The Buddha traveled all around India spreading the teachings and showing his followers how they could awaken. The sangha grew until thousands were practicing the Four Noble Truths. This chapter looks at the end of Buddha's life, and how the sangha grew and spread throughout India and beyond. These beginnings, supported by great kings, helped to establish what is now called Buddhism.

THE BUDDHA'S FINAL DAYS

The Buddha lived to be eighty years old. It was a time of unrest in India and the king of Magadha, Ajatasattu, had planned an offensive against the republics to the east of his kingdom, determined to wipe them out. The Buddha had decided to avoid the carnage and headed north to the margins of the Ganges basin. As death approached and the Buddha prepared to leave this world, he lived a life of increasing solitude, searching out places of quiet and peace. He was ill and was intent on making sure the sangha knew everything they needed to know before he departed this world.

A Simple Life

It might be easy to imagine the Buddha surrounded by riches and adored by many, much as some religious leaders are today. However, the Buddha remained a mendicant monk, and he frequently lived outside, among the mango groves, begging for his meals. He also spent a lot of time in the palace of his childhood friend, the then King

Pasenadi of Kosola. He and the sangha also dwelled in structures built specifically for them to spend the rainy seasons, the three-month monsoon that visits India each year.

His demise was particularly upsetting to his long-time companion Ananda. Ananda wanted to know who would take over for the Buddha, who would be the next in line to continue the teachings. But the Buddha knew that no one needed to take over. Each person would be a "light unto himself." By practicing the principles the Buddha had set forth, each could become self-reliant and work toward awakening. The sangha did not need an authority figure. The Buddha had taught them all they needed to know.

Final Days

The Buddha was growing weak and tired. He was ready to let go of his life. It can be inferred that he made a conscious decision to die when he ate some tainted pork, but he did not allow others who had received the offering to do so. While the story of eating tainted pork is widely recounted, the Buddha may have actually died from a more serious medical condition, one that the contaminated food worsened.

Teacher of Kings

S.N. Goenka says in the introduction to the Pali Canon that the Buddha gave teachings to hundreds of thousands during his dhamma (dharma) wanderings (*carika*). He was also pragmatic and political in his teachings, giving counsel to kings, for example: "The king should protect his subjects in the same way as he protects his own children." And, of course, he inspired the great King Ashoka to implement a righteous rule.

He reminded the sangha that he had only taught them things he himself had experienced and had taken nothing on the word of another. He told them to do the same. They should practice the disciplines he had taught them and should always, most important of all, live for others with lovingkindness and compassion for the entire world.

The Buddha partook of his last meal, a meal of spoiled meat given to him by a blacksmith named Chunda. Chunda placed the meat into the Buddha's alms bowl, and out of gratitude the Buddha ate it. The Buddha insisted that no one else present eat the meat he ingested, and he made them dispose of it after he was finished. In order that Chunda not feel responsible for the Buddha's illness and impending death, the Buddha called Chunda to his side and told him how grateful he was for the meal.

Dying Buddha

Reclining Buddha statues represent the Buddha on his deathbed. The Buddha said, "Each of you should make himself an island, make himself and no one else his refuge; each of you must make the dharma his island, the dharma and nothing else his refuge." Some of these statues are quite large and beautiful such as the Manuha Paya in Burma from the ninth century.

The Buddha, ill with food poisoning, traveled on to his eventual death site, Kushinagara. He then asked the sangha if they had any questions for him, if there was anything yet they did not understand. Right up until the end of his life, the Buddha served others and thought only of what the sangha needed. But no one came forth to ask any questions.

The Buddha then asked if perhaps they were not asking questions for which they needed answers out of reverence for him. If this was the case, he said, they could ask their questions through a friend. When still no one came forth the Buddha knew they were well versed in his teachings and, as Karen Armstrong tells us in *Buddha*, he uttered his last words: "All individual things pass away. Seek your liberation with diligence."

The Buddha died after teaching the dharma for forty-five years. Crowds gathered around the great sage to witness his passing and hear his last words. It is said he died with a smile on his face.

The Buddha was cremated according to custom and his remains were distributed amongst his followers along with other relics and enshrined in stupas. You can still visit some of these relics in India today. While the Buddha did not present himself as the founder of a religion, his relics and pilgrimage sights have been treated as holy for the past 2,500 years.

In India, Tibet, and Southeast Asian countries, stupas are usually dome-shaped with a center spire. In China, Korea, and Japan they became multitiered structures known as pagodas. They have traditionally been regarded as places of peace, sending out pacifying energies into their surroundings.

The Followers

The Buddha had taught his students well. His emphasis on self-reliance left the sangha in good shape. He had left behind his teachings, the dharma; and the sangha knew the dharma would guide them if they followed it.

However, shortly after the Buddha's death, one of the newly ordained bhikkus, Subhadda, rebelled. He suggested that now that the Buddha was gone—the one who oppressed them by telling them how to do this, how to do that—they had the freedom to do whatever they desired. They had the freedom to choose.

One of the Buddha's greatest students, the Venerable Mahakassapa, became very upset at Subhadda's statement. He decided that a council should be called to recite aloud all the Buddha's teachings. He knew well that if they did not establish the Buddha's teachings soon, it would not take long for all to be corrupted and lost.

THE COUNCILS

Establishing the Canon

According to the modern-day edition of the Pali Canon, over the past 2,500 years there have been six Dhamma (Dharma in Sanskrit) Councils (*Dhamma-Sangitas*) or "Dhamma Recitations." The process was as follows: "The basic teaching of the Buddha were first recited by an elder monk and then chanted after him in chorus by the whole assembly. The recitation was considered to be authentic when it was unanimously approved by all of the monks in attendance." The recitations were committed to writing at the Fourth Council some 500 years after the Buddha's death.

THE FIRST COUNCIL: THE COUNCIL AT RAJAGRIHA

Three months after the Buddha's death, 500 senior monks (arhats) gathered together at Rajagriha in what has come to be known as the First Council. Rajagriha was the capital of Magadha, which was one of the four great kingdoms (in addtition to Kosala, Vansa, and Avanti) in ancient India. Their hope was that they would be able to establish the Buddhist canon and create the definite teachings of the Buddha.

Ananda and Upali each took on a special task at the council. Ananda, as the longtime companion of the Buddha, was responsible for the recitation of the Buddha's teachings. It was felt that since he had spent so many years by the Buddha's side, he would have heard the teachings most frequently. Upali was given the task of setting forth the rules of discipline for the sangha (*vinaya*).

Worthy One

Arhat means "worthy one" in Sanskrit. An arhat is one who has attained enlightened mind and is free of desires and cravings. An arhat has nothing more to learn and has absorbed all of the Buddha's teachings.

Each of the arhats recited the teachings, examining the words to ensure they were accurate. They recited them over and over again, and each repetition was checked to make sure they all agreed that it was correct. The First Council lasted seven months.

The members of the council carried the memorized teachings away with them to all parts of the country, wherever disciples of the Buddha were to be found. Thus, the oral tradition of passing on the Buddha's teaching was established and remained so for many hundreds of years.

THE SECOND COUNCIL: THE COUNCIL AT VESALI

One hundred years after the First Council, the Second Council took place to settle disagreements regarding the monastic rules. This council was held at Vaishali (Vesali) and 700 arhats attended. The elders of the council felt that certain members of the sangha were taking some of the Ten Precepts (the Five Precepts for ethical living, plus additional precepts) too lightly and that there was a general slackening of discipline.

A group of monks put forth a series of changes in the precepts, making them more lax than they had been previously. For example, they felt it was acceptable for the members of the sangha to accept money, and they debated the need for the precept that forbade them to use money.

The assembly of monks thereby discussed the validity of the Ten Precepts. The dissenting monks, the Vajjians, were outvoted. They refused to give in, however, and seceded from the group of the council of elders. Thus, Buddhism was divided into two schools of thought: Theravada and Mahayana. The elders belonged to the Theravada school; Vajjian monks split off to create the Mahayana school, which differed in the interpretation of the precepts and philosophy.

KING ASHOKA AND THE THIRD COUNCIL: THE COUNCIL AT PATALIPUTRA

The Third Council convened in 326 B.C.E. with 1,000 monks working on it for nine months. The need for this council arose as debate was being carried on about both the dharma and the precepts. At this time, King Ashoka was ruling a vast empire in India, created by his grandfather Chadragupta Maurya in the wake of Alexander the Great. He had taken the throne in a bloody war and was a ruthless leader with many violent triumphs to his credit. But during the eighth year of his rule, after a particularly gruesome battle at

Kalinga, King Ashoka became shaken by the bloodbath—upward of 100,000 people are said to have been slaughtered—that set the stage for a powerful change within Ashoka.

Ashoka and the Spread of Buddhism

King Ashoka was largely responsible for the spread of Buddhism beyond India's borders and its emergence as one of the world's great religions. He sent emissaries as far as Greece to the west and China to the east. He practiced tolerance and respect for other religious disciplines, promoted peace instead of war, and established schools, hospitals, and orphanages for his people. He was living proof that it is possible to rule a great nation with kindness and open-mindedness, promoting peace and goodwill.

Ashoka ran into a monk who told the mighty king that he could use his power for good instead of evil. The monk was a Buddhist. Ashoka soon exchanged his sword for the dharma.

He stopped hunting and fighting, and started meditating and doing humanitarian work. Instead of soldiers he had missionary monks, who spread the dharma wherever they could, reaching out past the boundaries of India and into the neighboring nations. He built 84,000 stupas and thousands of monasteries throughout the land. King Ashoka inscribed his new beliefs on rocks that can be found throughout India, Nepal, Pakistan, and Afghanistan.

These inscriptions would come to be known as the Edicts of King Ashoka and included such promises as moderate spending, proper schooling for children, medical treatments for everyone, and promotion of proper behavior. He promised to practice the dharma until the end of time, to always be available—no matter what he was doing—for the affairs of his people; he promoted respect for everyone and all religions.

Living by His Principles

"Dharma is good. But what does dharma consist of? It consists of a few sins and many good deeds, of kindness, liberality, truthfulness, and purity." So said Ashoka, and he expected his officials to live according to these principles (imagine if Congress ran like this?). Ashoka was a *dharmaraja* (just king), a chakravartin monarch who promoted the dharma through his rule and example.

Because he practiced such spiritual generosity, many less-devoted practitioners entered the Buddhist practice and the purity of the practice was diluted. Ashoka sought to weed out these weak links from the monasteries he had created and called a new council with the genuine, steadfast monks who were left.

At the Third Council, the teachings were reviewed and a new, purified collection was set forth. Nine missions of arhats were sent out to spread the dharma into different areas of India and across its vast borders into other countries.

THE FOURTH COUNCIL: ONE NORTH, ONE SOUTH

There were two Fourth Councils. One is believed to have taken place in Sri Lanka in 29 B.C.E. with 500 monks writing down the orally transmitted teachings for the first time. Another council is said to have been held in India in the first century C.E. This council was led by Kanishka, ruler of what is today Pakistan and northern India. King Kanishka loved the teachings of the Buddha and often had bhikkus in to teach him the dharma.

He soon found that they were not in accord on the teaching of the dharma, and he was very distressed over the differences he heard. At the advice of another, he convened a council to sort out the differences. Five hundred monks compiled a new canon at the Fourth Council.

This was the start of the Mahayana scriptural canon: the collection of Mahayana teachings. Theravada Buddhists, however, do not recognize this council.

In the Theravada tradition, the Fifth Council took place in Mandalay, Burma, in 1871. Two thousand, four hundred monks labored for five months inscribing the Tipitaka ("Three Baskets") onto marble slabs. The Sixth Council took place in Rangoon in 1954, with 2,500 monks from all the Theravada countries.

EARLY BUDDHISM

Scriptures and Divisions

During the time of the Second Council, Buddhism started to splinter into different schools of thought. Then, as the dharma spread to other countries and cultures at the time of King Ashoka, different traditions arose. There arose the Hinayana and the Mahayana traditions. Hinayana was the tradition that spread under King Ashoka.

Hinayana refers to a group of eighteen Buddhist schools, of which only one is currently in existence, Theravada. Mahayana Buddhists, who called their tradition "the Great Vehicle," named the other traditions of Buddhism "Hinayana"—meaning "Little Vehicle"—which is not considered a favorable term by many Buddhists. Today you would not use the word Hinayana to refer to the Theravada tradition of Buddhism.

THE PALI CANON

One version of the canon in the original Pali language has been published by the Pali Text Society in England; the other is published by the Vipassana Research Institute in India. These volumes represent the teachings of the Buddha. Known as the *pitakas* ("baskets"), the Pali Canon was written down on palm leaves at the Fourth Council and was thus passed down intact to future generations of scholars and the sangha. These original transcripts have since been lost.

The canon consists of the three "baskets." The *Vinaya* (monastic code of discipline) covers daily practices on how to maintain harmony among the monks and nuns. The *Suttas* (the popular discourses) contains the collection of the central teachings of Theravada Buddhism, including all the Jataka tales, the *Dhammapada*, and various discourses. There are more than 10,000 discourses. The third basket is the *Abhidhamma* that are manuals of Buddhist psychology compiled after the life of the Buddha from his teachings in the suttas.

Spread of Theravada Buddhism

Theravada Buddhism spread to Burma, Cambodia, Laos, Sri Lanka, and Thailand. Mahayana spread to China, Japan, Korea, Mongolia, Nepal, Russia, Tibet, and Vietnam. The Theravada that survives today was derived from the elder monks at the Second Council.

The discourses typically start with, "Thus I have heard . . ." to emphasize the direct link to the Buddha. Also noted are the location and the audience the Buddha was addressing. The sutta (sutra) section of the Pali Canon includes the Digha Nikaya (Long Discourses), Maijhima Nikaya (Medium-Length Discourses), Samyutta Nikaya (Connected Discourses), Anguttara Nikaya (Numbered Discourses), and Khuddaka Nikaya (Small Texts).

The Abhidhamma is "a compendium of profound teachings elucidating the functioning and interrelationships of mind, mental factors, matter, and the phenomenon transcending these." In Pali, *abhi* means "ultimate," so Abhidhamma meant the "ultimate truth," or ultimate teachings. The Abhidhamma can be thought of as a view of the world from the perspective of ultimate enlightenment.

The Pitaka was the written version of the oral tradition that persisted at the time of the Buddha and in the years after his death.

Recitation of the canon persisted even after it was written down and continues to do so to this day. Over the centuries, the Pali Canon has been preserved in Burma, Sri Lanka, Thailand, and Cambodia. The versions that emerged in these different countries are meaningfully the same, attesting to the validity of their contents.

MAHAYANA SCRIPTURES

The Mahayana Buddhists had their own scriptures, which were written in Sanskrit. These texts included:

1. Sutras (the words of the Buddha): including the Heart Sutra, the Lotus Sutra, and the Diamond Sutra.
2. Shastras: the commentary on the sutras.
3. Tantras: mystical texts.

As Mahayana Buddhism grew, new texts were added. The Mahayana asserts that emptiness (similar to anatta or "no self") permeates everything and that the earlier texts were not explicit enough on this point, a criticism of the Abhidharma. The Mahayana asserts that nothing is fixed—everything is empty, including nirvana. Nirvana is not a thing that can be attained. All concepts can lead to attachment and thus become a pitfall preventing you from experiencing *prajnaparamita* ("perfection of wisdom"). The Mahayana sutras explore such themes as emptiness.

The Lotus Sutra is another prominent Mahayana text that was very influential in China. The oldest surviving copy was translated in 286 C.E. The Lotus Sutra, in contrast to the Heart Sutra, is a long discourse with twenty-eight chapters. According to Professor Mark Blum, the Lotus Sutra covers three themes:

- A universal path to liberation
- The eternal nature of the Buddha
- Pragmatism represented by the bodhisattva

The Parable of the Burning House appears in the Lotus Sutra. Children are playing in a burning house and they don't heed their father's warning to escape because they are so enthralled with the game they are playing. Their attachment to the game represents the dangerous attachment to greed and desire. The father entices them out with a promise of better entertainment but then gives them jewels and bells. These represent the dharma.

Nagarjuna

The second most influential person in the history of Buddhism is Nagarjuna (the Buddha being the first). He founded the Madhyamika ("School of the Middle Way"). He cautioned that dualistic ways of perceiving are limiting and took the Buddha's notion of dependent origination (that is, nothing exists except in relationship to something else, and thus everything is interconnected) to its logical conclusion whereby the difference between nirvana and samsara disappears.

Today there are different traditions of Buddhism, just as there were in the past. In fact, the three major surviving traditions within Buddhism can be considered related but distinct religions: Theravada, Mahayana (for example, Zen), and Vajrayana (for example, Tibetan Buddhism).

THERAVADA AND MAHAYANA

Emerging Traditions

Theravada Buddhism can be traced all the way back to the First Council, shortly after Buddha's death. Theravada Buddhists claim that they have adhered to the Buddha's original teachings and are, therefore, the purist form of Buddhism. They established the Pali Canon, the teachings that were passed down orally for four hundred years. The Pali language is still used as the primary language for the texts of Theravada Buddhists millennia later.

The Theravada ("Doctrine of Elders") is the sole surviving school of Buddhism from the early days of Buddhism. It traces its roots back to the Buddha himself and his closest disciples. It is also known as southern Buddhism because this is where it has flourished over the centuries: Sri Lanka, Thailand, Burma, Cambodia, and Laos. Theravada keeps its ties close to the life of the Buddha and the Pali Canon (unlike Mahayana, which has introduced new texts and concepts).

The Theravada forms that have made their way to America, especially, are more "Buddha" than "Buddhism." That is, they preserve the essential practices the Buddha developed and taught and most closely resemble his path to awakening. Notably, meditation is central to the Theravada traditions taught in America, where interested parties can learn meditation through a traditional ten-day silent meditation retreat. Here you can engage in the core Buddhist practice of vipassana without having to engage with any rites or rituals, or take any monastic vows. It's more of a bare bones practice of Buddha and can be found in the teachings of S.N. Goenka from Burma who founded the Vipassana Meditation Society, which has centers in the US and all around the world, the Insight Meditation

Society in Barre, Massachusetts, and its sister non-residential center, Cambridge Insight Meditation Center, and the Spirit Rock Meditation Center in California.

MAHAYANA

Mahayana Buddhism is the vehicle most familiar to Americans in the form of Zen. Mahayana has been around since the Second Council, but Mahayana also can argue a direct descent to the Buddha's teachings. Mahayana Buddhists believe they split off from the Theravada tradition in order to reform the teachings and take them back to a purer form the Buddha had originally taught, although the Mahayana sutras such as the Perfection of Wisdom and Heart Sutra are not directly attributed to the Buddha.

Manjushri

Manjushri is the bodhisattva of wisdom—he symbolizes the wisdom one needs to seek the truth. In artworks depicting Manjushri, he is often portrayed with one hand holding a sword, which is needed to cut through illusion to the heart of wisdom. In the other hand, he holds the sacred text of wisdom, the Prajnaparamita Sutra.

If you think Buddhism lacks prophecies, think again. Buddhist scholar Mark Blum describes the Mahayana belief in the Period of the Final Law. This period of dark decline for humanity (know as *mofa* in Chinese and *mappo* in Japanese) had come about somewhere between the sixth and eleventh centuries "because too much time had elapsed since the death of the Buddha and fewer and fewer people understood his teaching." Blum explains, "This final period could last up to ten thousand years and all sorts of dire consequences were described, such as increased corruption, conflict, and even a shortening of human life. But the end of this age was unambiguously marked by the advent of a new buddha, Maitreya, who will usher in a new era of peace and enlightenment."

Emptiness

The cardinal emphasis of Mahayana is on *shunyata*, often translated as "emptiness" or "the void." The Buddha's early teachings discuss the emptiness of self (anatman, anatta) and in the Mahayana this concept is expanded to everything.

Shunyata is, perhaps, the most confusing and mystical of the Buddhist concepts and the most difficult for the Western mind to grasp. Truth goes beyond dualistic distinctions and thus "emptiness is form" and "form is emptiness."

These distinctions can get you bogged down in subtle philosophical arguments. Is the world real? And what does it mean to be real? To further clarify things (or is it to complicate things?) objects can be seen as conventionally real but there is an ultimate reality that underlies what is perceived. Confused yet?

In Mahayana tradition, when one wakes up one realizes that the *whole world* is emptiness, that emptiness is not just the self but all things, and form and emptiness are the same thing, indistinguishable from one another. Or as it states in the Heart Sutra: "Form is emptiness, emptiness is form." It is hard to grasp this conceptually. The best way is to practice meditation and experience it for yourself.

Like the self, everything has the quality of space and energy and change.

Stephen Batchelor tries to cut through this confusion by going back to basics. According to Batchelor, the Buddha's original teachings did not make these distinctions between relative and ultimate reality (which themselves are at risk for creating a duality). Things are constantly changing, he taught, and he cautioned his followers not to cling to anything. Everything that occurs does so in dependence upon something else (the doctrine of dependent origination).

But is there really a duality here? Conventional reality is necessary so that you know your name and know how to find your way home. Ultimate reality refers to something else. When you meditate, you will experience these conventional things in a different way—this is where language breaks down—such that some deeper or more ultimate sense of things will be experienced.

It's hard to describe in language and must be experienced for yourself. When all these concepts cease to function, you have reached enlightenment. When you go beyond dualistic categories such as self and world, you are liberated. This is what the Mahayana strives for. The aim is to get beyond all your preconceived notions of reality, including those about yourself. Beware! You can become attached to the concept of emptiness itself, and through the back door you will once again be trapped in the world of concepts and miss out on liberation. Don't worry though. Of course, in the next moment you'll have another chance!

Vipassana practice plays a more central role in the Theravada than in the Mahayana where *vipashyana* (Sanskrit for vipassana) is combined with elaborate imagery, chanting, and other practices that developed in the centuries after the Buddha. In the Mahayana, prajna (wisdom) may be represented by Manjushri who yields a sword that cuts through delusion and desire.

Ox-Herding Pictures

The Mahayana Path is captured in the traditional sequence of painting in the Chan and Zen traditions. The ox, an animal sacred in India, represents buddha-nature, and the boy in the illustrations represents the self.

- "Seeking the Ox." Here you are lost in samsara but having been exposed to the teaching of the Buddha you are pulled toward a higher truth.
- "Finding the Tracks." Here you engage with listening to teachings and finding the path.
- "First Glimpse of the Ox." Meditation practice provides the vehicle to start realizing a taste of prajna (wisdom).
- "Catching the Ox." Comes when you have a deeper grasping of the kleshas or three fires (ignorance, greed, hatred), and the limitations that come with regarding the self as a solid object worthy of protection (anatta).
- "Taming the Ox." This occurs when you start to have peeks at the peak experience of *satori* (seeing into one's true nature; awakening).
- "Riding the Ox Home." When you have a complete experience of satori.
- "Ox Forgotten." This comes when you can now experience life with the freedom that satori provides.
- "Both Ox and Self Forgotten." Here you go beyond even the concepts of dharma and the tradition you studied within. The Buddha likened this to the raft that carries you across the river of samsara; once you've reached the other side you don't keep carrying the raft.
- "Returning to the Source." From this place you realize that the entire natural world is the embodiment of enlightenment.
- "Entering the Market with Helping Hands." Makes the bodhisattva path explicit. Having gotten to this place you now work for the betterment of everyone else.

THE SPREAD OF BUDDHISM

Beyond India

Buddhist practice spread quickly within India as the Buddha and his disciples traveled around the country introducing the dharma to the population. The power of his message and the proof of its value were evident as thousands joined the sangha. "Followers of the Buddha" were soon to be found beyond the borders of India in Sri Lanka, Southeast Asia, and beyond. Eventually what is now called "Buddhism" spread to China, Korea, Japan, and Tibet.

SRI LANKA

Remember that monks were mendicants—they had few possessions. They traveled by foot, begging for food, mingling amongst the native people while performing compassionate acts to further themselves along the path toward enlightenment. As they traveled they spread the message of the Buddha's teachings and convinced people—through example rather than self-promotion—that the Path was a good way to live. Their passage through south Asia was one way in which Buddhism started to spread across the continent.

King Ashoka Sends His Son

Also recall that King Ashoka was another primary reason for the spread and growth of Buddhism. Ashoka was the great Buddhist missionary. Powerful and respected, Ashoka attracted people to the Buddha's teaching through his missions and architectural monuments throughout his kingdom.

Meditation is often practiced by Buddhist monks. Meditation clarifies the senses, concentrates the mind, and calms the emotions. All of these aspects of meditation are part of the path to enlightenment.

About 2,500 years ago and according to legend, Siddhartha, an Indian prince, meditated beneath the Bodhi Tree for three days and nights. He achieved enlightenment and became the Buddha. Some 300 years later, the ruler of a vast Indian empire, King Ashoka, converted to Buddhism and ordered the construction of the Mahabodhi Temple on the site of Siddhartha's enlightenment. Today, in addition to being a Buddhist temple, the Mahabodhi Temple in Bodh Gaya, India, is a UNESCO World Heritage Site.

The lotus flower is a symbol of Buddhism. Because it grows in muddy water, it shows that the purity of enlightenment can arise out of murkiness. It is the aim of Buddhists to attain a state of enlightenment through meditation and lovingkindness. Water slips off the flower's petals easily, mirroring Buddhism's notion of detachment from the desires of this world.

This 112-foot-high statue of the Buddha at the Po Lin Monastery in Hong Kong is characteristic of many representations of the Buddha. Here, as in most other images, the Buddha is seated, radiating an atmosphere of calm and lovingkindness. The statue was completed in 1993.

A Buddhist tea ceremony (*chanoyu* in Japanese) is an elaborate ritual designed to give its participants an opportunity to meditate and focus their minds. The tea is made in a series of predetermined steps, as the host concentrates on each aspect of the preparation. Each of the guests in turn drinks from the bowl in which the tea has been prepared. After all the guests have drunk, the host washes the bowl in cold water.

Photo Credit: © Getty Images/DavorLovincic

Buddhists often use prayer beads during worship to keep track of the number of times a mantra is said. Generally, a string of beads is looped around the wrist for convenience. In most cases, 108 beads are in a string, and they are said to symbolize the number of desires to which humans are subject. When all of the beads have been counted, the devotee is considered to have said one hundred mantras (the other eight are if she loses her place and misses some beads). The beads can be made of various materials, including wood, precious or semiprecious stones, or seeds.

Photo Credit: © Getty Images/guenterguni

Candles, incense, and a singing bowl are often used by Buddhists when meditating. Singing bowls create a range of sounds that can calm the mind of the person meditating, helping him or her relax and focus on the immediacy of the moment through regular breathing and concentration. The steady, unwavering light of the candles and the smell of the incense also provide calming influences.

Photo Credit: © Getty Images/VeraPetruk

Frescoes from the Lankatilaka Vihara Buddhist temple in Sri Lanka. The temple dates from the fourteenth century and is considered one of the most architecturally significant structures of its period. It is unique in that it was constructed atop a great rock; the foundations are of granite on which bricks were laid to create the temple. The frescoes depict worshipers at a statue of the Buddha.

Photo Credit: © Getty Images/fmajor

Mandalas are intended as maps of the spiritual world. The patterns within them represent the sacred space where the Buddha resides. A mandala can serve as the focal point of a meditation. The person meditating concentrates on the colors and shapes in order to exclude everything else from her mind. Many mandalas are created from different colors of sand. When the meditation is complete, the sand is swept away, reminding those meditating that nothing is permanent.

In ancient times, a great Buddhist school and monastery existed at Nalanda in India. Scholars who studied there helped shape Buddhist doctrine. At its height, Nalanda had a vast library that included books not only about religion but about grammar, mathematics, history, and many other subjects. As well, the library included key Buddhist texts such as the Prajnaparamita Sutras and the Guhyasamaja Tantra.

Gardening is particularly connected to Japanese Zen Buddhism. The garden provides a peaceful place for meditation. In gardens such as this one in Japan, ponds often contain floating lotus flowers symbolic of Buddhism.

The Tiger's Nest monastery in Bhutan is situated 3,000 feet above the Paro Valley and more than 10,000 feet above sea level. The prayer flags in the foreground are typical of Himalayan Buddhism. They are hung in long strings; the five colors appear in the same order: blue, white, red, green, and yellow. Blue symbolizes the sky; white the air; red, fire; green, water; and yellow, earth.

Photo Credit: © Getty Images/narvikk

Yoga has become widely popular in the West. The Buddha was a practiced yogi, seeking to yoke mind and body, future and past together. Because Buddhism is concerned with promoting mindfulness of all actions, Buddhist yogis concentrate on being aware of their bodies and their breathing much more than getting a workout. Through yoga, by focusing on sitting calmly and being aware of all their movements, Buddhists find ways to explore their inner being and consciousness.

Photo Credit: © Getty Images/shironosov

King Ashoka had cast his eye toward the south and decided to send his son, the monk Mahinda, to the beautiful tropical island Sri Lanka as a missionary. Mahinda was well received by King Devanampiyatissa, the king of Sri Lanka, and they held many enthusiastic and energetic conversations about the religion that had so completely changed Ashoka.

Indian Buddhism's Decline

After its glory days under King Ashoka, Buddhism in India took a downturn. The invasions by the Mongols, an Islamic people, and the resurgence and strengthening of Hinduism (in part due to a repopularization after incorporating elements of Buddhism) were to take a toll on the influence of Buddhism. By the thirteenth century, Buddhism was substantially weakened in India and all but disappeared. Fortunately, it was to take a stronghold in other parts of the world, a thriving that continued to the modern era.

Captivated by such engaging exchanges, the native king asked Mahinda to bring a branch of the Bodhi Tree to Sri Lanka so they could have their own symbol of enlightenment. And so Mahinda sent for his sister, Sanghamitta, who soon left India for Sri Lanka, bearing the gift her brother had requested. A grateful King Devanampiyatissa planted the branch on the grounds of the Mahavihara—the first and largest monastery built in the city of Anuradhapura. To this day there are Bodhi Trees in Sri Lanka considered to be relatives to the original branch brought over by Sanghamitta.

Sri Lanka embraced Buddhism and shortly it was thriving in the small nation. Sometime around 100 B.C.E., it was here during the Fourth Council that the Pali scriptures were written down on palm leaves.

Sri Lanka Nurtures Buddhism

Some four hundred years later, in the fifth century a Buddhist monk named Buddhaghosa left India for the beautiful island. Buddhaghosa wrote a detailed examination of the Tipitaka, a commentary on the Pali texts, called *Visuddhimagga* (Path to Purity). It is still widely read today and is considered the great treatise of Theravada Buddhism. In Pali, Buddhaghosa means "Voice of Enlightenment." He was also known as The Great Translator.

During the fourth century C.E., the Buddha's tooth was brought to Sri Lanka with great fanfare. To this day there is a celebration centered around the Buddha's tooth. It is preserved in the city of Kandy in the Temple of the Tooth Relic. Daily rituals revolve around the venerated tooth; it is a much revered and celebrated artifact.

Buddhism was eventually challenged by European colonialism and invasions of the Portuguese, the Dutch, and the British. Efforts to convert the natives to Christianity were exerted but Buddhist practice persisted. At one point bhikkus were imported from India to retain and fortify the presence of Buddhism. Buddhism prevailed, and today Sri Lanka is considered one of the few predominantly Buddhist countries.

MYANMAR (BURMA)

From Sri Lanka and India, Buddhism continued its march across the Asian continent. Monks from Sri Lanka left their home to spread the teachings abroad, having a powerful impact on such other countries as Burma, Thailand, Laos, and Cambodia. These southeastern transmissions were in the Theravada tradition. Buddhism originally came to Burma via trade with the people of India and via monks from Sri

Lanka. With the aid of Sri Lankan monks and supporters, Buddhism established a firm foothold.

Originally in Burma the predominant form of Buddhism was Vajrayana Buddhism, but by the year 1044 the powerful Burmese king Anawrahta sponsored Theravada monasteries and changed the country to a largely Theravada-supported nation. Anawrahta built monasteries, stupas, and shrines all over the capital city of Pagan, and the city soon became a center for Buddhist study and practice.

Buddhism flourished in Burma for many years, but ran up against a large threat with the British invasion of the nineteenth century. Today Theravada Buddhism continues to flourish. There are more than 50,000 monasteries to be found and fully 88 percent of the population considers themselves Buddhist.

THAILAND

Buddhism is said to have first appeared in Thailand among the Mon people in the third century B.C.E. The Mons left China about 2,000 years ago and settled in both Thailand and Burma. They are believed to be the first settlers in Thailand. Once established, they soon encountered other peoples arriving from the north. Many small kingdoms were subsequently established across the land, each vying for power over another. It is likely—considering the first settlers were from China—that some Chinese Buddhist influence was possible. However, Buddhism is generally considered to have appeared in Thailand from India and not from China.

By the thirteenth century, missionaries from Sri Lanka were able to convince the king of Thailand, Ramkhamhaeng, to convert to Buddhism. Pali was established as the religious language of Thailand and Theravada Buddhism firmly took root, where it thrives to this day.

There was a revival of the Theravadan traditions in the nine-teenth and twentieth centuries across Southeast Asia. In Burma and Sri Lanka these reforms were part of the independence movement against colonial rule. In Thailand, which retained its independence, reform was initiated by King Rama IV (reign 1851–1868) who was a monk himself for twenty-seven years.

CAMBODIA, LAOS, AND INDONESIA

From India, Buddhism spread to the east and south.

Cambodia

Cambodia was influenced by India early in its history and Mahayana Buddhism took a foothold with its people. Early Cambodian history is not well documented, so it is not until the ninth century that we know Buddhism was being practiced there. Kings of the Khmer, who were dominant in Cambodia, started to build large temples and monasteries.

Buddhism in Southeast Asia

Buddhism has exerted influence on Southeast Asia since the first century and has taken a predominately Theravada form (except in Vietnam). Great material and political resources were devoted to building what are now some of the world's most magnificent ruins: Angkor in Cambodia, Pagan in Burma, and Borobudur in Java.

Then at the turn of the twelfth century, King Jayavarman VII came into power. He was a devout Buddhist and Mahayana Buddhism became the dominant religion of the kingdom under his influence. Neighbor Thailand was soon to have a strong effect, however, and by the end of the thirteenth century Theravada was predominant.

When Pol Pot and the Khmer Rouge guerillas took control of Cambodia in the 1970s they tried to eradicate Buddhism and nearly succeeded. There were 65,000 monks in the sangha before 1970, and after Pol Pot, that number was 3,000. Approximately two-thirds of the Buddhist temples were destroyed. Today Buddhism is attempting to re-establish itself but political unrest continues. There has been resurgence in the sangha and 95 percent of the population is Theravada Buddhist.

Laos

As in Cambodia, Laotian Buddhism was probably introduced by the Khmer. Later, it was heavily influenced by Thailand and thusly became Buddhist in the Theravada school. Communists also tried to rid Laos of Buddhism in 1975, and a large percentage of the sangha fled the country. The remaining religious communities were under strict state control. Recent reforms and dialogues are moving to declare Theravada Buddhism the state religion. Fully 60 percent of the population is considered to be practicing Buddhists.

Indonesia

The first Buddhists arrived in Indonesia sometime in the first century from India. It is believed that Buddhism spread here through Ashoka's missionaries as well. Both Theravada and Mahayana Buddhism were prevalent, though Mahayana eventually took hold in the eighth century C.E. In the ninth century, the largest Buddhist shrine in the world was built on the island of Java. It is known as Borobudur, and this monumental stupa was most likely built at the end of the ninth century by Hindu kings as a central sanctuary of the Buddhist religion. Until recent history, Borobudur was mostly covered and just a small portion was visible above the surrounding earth and forests. It was restored just two hundred years ago. This enormous temple is said to be a mandala, a representation of the cosmos, constructed by practicing tantric Buddhists.

NORTHWARD BOUND

Mahayana Buddhism was spreading northward from India as Theravada was spreading throughout the south and southeast. Vajrayana Buddhism headed north to Tibet and took a fast hold of that isolated mountainous country. Mahayana Buddhism proliferated in China, Japan, and Korea.

The Silk Road

Silk was a hot commodity in the ancient world, and in the second century B.C.E., routes developed across Asia that allowed the passage of silk and other goods from one country to another. The main route, which came to be known as the Silk Road, was just north of India and west of Tibet. The 6,000-mile road traversed what would be Afghanistan, Pakistan, and northwestern China today.

The Silk Road connected India to China. Silk and other goods went one way and gold and silver went the other. Early Chinese tradesmen started to hear of the wonderful teachings coming out of India and curiosity in Buddhism was aroused in China. The first missionaries to China arrived in the first century C.E. They headed northward from India to spread the teachings of the Buddha. Literate Chinese started translating the sutras into Chinese and continued to do so for eight centuries.

FARTHER EAST

Expansion Continues

Monks headed over the footpaths of the Himalaya Mountains into remote and isolated Tibet, taking their Buddhist practices with them. They reached Tibet and began to spread the teachings, as so many others were doing all over Southeast Asia. But it wasn't until the seventh century, when the king of Tibet, Songtsen Gambo, married two Buddhist women—one a princess from Nepal and the other a princess from China—that Buddhism flourished in Tibet. It wasn't long before the king became very interested in Buddhism, sending representatives from Tibet over to China and India to learn more about it.

He became convinced of the benefits of the Buddhist lifestyle and his faith strengthened. He built many temples and encouraged the growth of Buddhism among his people. Eventually Mahayana scriptures were translated into Tibetan. Buddhism remained a prominent part of life in Tibet until 1959, when the Dalai Lama went into exile in India after ten years of Chinese occupation.

KOREA

Buddhism arrived in Korea in 372. At that time shamanism—a religion based on nature worship and the belief in a world of gods, demons, and ancestral spirits—was the native religion. Buddhism would eventually blend in with shamanism to create Korean Buddhism. Shamanism promoted a belief in three gods: the god of the mountains, the hermit god, and the god of the seven stars. Korean

Buddhism blended the belief in these gods into the teachings of the Buddha, and Korean Buddhism blossomed.

Pure Land and Son (Korean Zen or Chan) also found their way to Korea and took root there. Son emphasized meditation practice over text study, and eventually nine different Son schools emerged in Korea, which were called the Nine Schools of Son.

Today about half the population of Korea is Buddhist, though Buddhism has deep roots in the community and many others incorporate Buddhist practices into their lives, regardless of religious affiliation.

THE EAST TODAY

Millennia ago Buddhism spread quickly over Asia and was soon well on its way to becoming a major world religion. Theravada Buddhism flourished in Sri Lanka, Cambodia, Laos, Thailand, Myanmar, and Bangladesh. Mahayana Buddhism had deep roots in Tibet, Japan, China, Korea, Vietnam, Indonesia, and Nepal. The twentieth century saw Buddhism emerge in the West, and now vital centers of Theravada, Zen, and Tibetan Buddhism are here in the United States.

Today, the top ten countries with the highest number of Buddhist practitioners are:

1. Thailand
2. Cambodia
3. Myanmar
4. Bhutan
5. Sri Lanka
6. Tibet

7. Laos
8. Vietnam
9. Japan
10. Macau

Although the countries with the greatest number of Buddhists are all in the Eastern hemisphere, Buddhism has made great inroads in the West. In the past fifty years, Americans and other Westerners have been increasingly interested in changing their lives through the practice of the dharma. Writers, philosophers, artists, and teachers have spread the word of Buddhism all over North America and Europe.

Refugees from Tibet have brought Buddhism into the public eye and the Dalai Lama tirelessly works with the hope of returning to his native Tibet. Emigrants from Asia have brought their practices westward and introduced new ideas and a new way of life into the hearts and minds of Americans and Europeans. Buddhism might be new to the West but the seeds of dharma have been firmly planted in Western soil.

VAJRAYANA

Tibetan Buddhism

Vajrayana Buddhism developed out of the Mahayana school of teachings sometime between the third and seventh centuries C.E. It is said that the Buddha practiced this esoteric tradition, but because of its advanced and special nature it didn't evolve into common practice. Vajrayana Buddhists believe the Buddha taught these practices through special texts, called tantras, but the tantras themselves didn't come to light until the seventh century.

Vajrayana Buddhists believe their teachings can be directly linked to the Buddha and that *they* practice the purest form of Buddhism. Vajrayana is found predominately in Tibet, a remote country, surrounded by the Himalaya Mountains and isolated from the rest of the world. Tibetan Buddhism emerged when Mahayana Buddhism reached Tibet and it became intertwined with the native Bön folk religion.

Other Names

Vajrayana Buddhism is also called Tantric Buddhism, "Diamond Vehicle," the "Completion Vehicle," the "Thunderbolt Vehicle," and the "Indestructible Path."

Tibet absorbed Buddhism into its culture wholeheartedly. According to Jack Maguire in *Essential Buddhism*, "No other country in history has absorbed this religion so thoroughly and, in turn, invested it with so much native character or so much cultural power. As Vajrayana grew increasingly influential in Tibet, so did the monastery as the focus of daily life, a position it retained until the mid-twentieth century . . . Over time, the monasteries assumed complete political control of the country, giving Tibet a singularly sacred form of government for centuries."

Vajrayana relies heavily on symbol and ritual, more so than other forms of Buddhism. It invokes magical deities belonging to a cosmic monastery. The practices in Vajrayana Buddhism are special and complex. The teachings are designed to bring the student to enlightenment in this lifetime; therefore, the practices are intense, subtle, difficult, and enlightenment presumably occurs more quickly than with other forms of practice. The student of the tantric practices has a teacher, called a guru (an enlightened teacher is a *lama*). The practices are often kept secret between the student and teacher, which adds to the mystery around the tradition.

VAJRAYANA'S TOOLBOX

The practices of Vajrayana revolve around a spiritual "toolbox" that contains such items as *mandalas, mantras, yidams, mudras,* and *vajras*.

Mandalas

Mandalas are maps of the spiritual world. They are usually represented in artwork as a symbolic pattern. The pattern is usually in the form of a circle with intricate designs within. The patterns are representative of the sacred place where the Buddha or deities abide. They are used for contemplation and meditation and are designed to guide the process of spiritual awakening.

Mantras

Mantras are mystical incantations whose repetitions contain the potential for spiritual connection. By repeating a mantra you can clear the mind and purify speech. The most famous mantra in Vajrayana is *Om mani padme hum*, which roughly translates to "Hail to the jewel in the lotus." Viewing the written mantra is also just as powerful as the incantation. You can also spin the written form of the mantra around in a prayer wheel, which is believed to have the same beneficial properties as chanting and viewing the written form.

What and Who Is a Dalai Lama?

The Dalai Lama is considered to be the present incarnation of the bodhisattva Avalokiteshvara. The third great leader of the Geluk lineage of Tibetan Buddhism was given the title Dalai Lama ("Ocean of Wisdom") and was deemed to be the physical manifestation of the compassionate bodhisattva. The present-day Dalai Lama is the fourteenth Dalai Lama.

Prayer wheels, also called *Mani* wheels by the Tibetans, are mechanical devices for dispersing spiritual blessings. Prayer wheels look like two wheels with an axle in between them. Paper with the mantra printed on it many times over is rolled around an axle of the wheel in a protective container. Tibetan Buddhists will circumambulate a stupa that contains dozens or even hundreds of these prayer wheels while chanting *Om mani padme hum* and spinning the wheels as they walk by. Some wheels are portable, with a handle, and some are much larger and stationary.

Yidam

Yidam are meditational deities. Tibetan art colorfully represents a multitude of spiritual deities, both male and female. They are considered to be different manifestations of the Buddha. Some of the yidam are actually wrathful deities. Tantric masters subdue these demons to subordinate them to the service of the Buddha.

Mudra

A mudra is the formation your hands take when meditating. The formation is deeply symbolic and often relates to a particular deity. A common mudra is the cosmic mudra:

The dominant hand is held palm up on your lap. The other hand is placed on top of the dominant hand so that the knuckles of both hands overlap. The thumbs touch lightly so that you are forming a circle.

Vajra

Vajra is a sanskrit term meaning thunderbolt. It is *dorje* in Tibetan and can be translated as "diamond" or "adamantine" referring to its indestructible qualities of emptiness. Vajras are symbolic, ritual objects such as a bell or dagger used in the manifold Tibetan ceremonies, rites, and rituals.

Vajrayana Practice

The student in Vajrayana Buddhism is called the *chela*. The chela is initiated into his practice by his guru. The chela is given a mandala of his prescribed yidam. Practice can be arduous. For example, in one practice a chela would undertake to make 100,000 prostrations and numerous repetitions of mantras.

THE SIX TRADITIONS

Tibetan Spirituality

Historically, there are six traditions, or schools, of Tibetan spirituality. Four of these schools are considered the principal schools. The six traditions are:

1. The Bön tradition.
2. The Nyingma tradition (the Old Ones).
3. The Bound by Command School (Kadam).
4. The Sakya tradition.
5. The Kagyu tradition (the Transmitted Command School).
6. The Gelug tradition (the Virtuous School).

The four principal schools are: Nyingma, Sakya, Kagyu, and Gelug.

THE BÖN TRADITION

The Bön tradition is alive today and getting stronger after a long period of virtual invisibility in Tibet during the eighth to the eleventh centuries. The Bön community has been successful in establishing monasteries in India and Nepal. It is an integral part of Tibetan culture and history, and the Tibetans strive to preserve Bön customs.

The five other traditions of Tibetan spirituality are all Buddhist and combine elements of all three vehicles of Buddhism—Theravada, Mahayana, and Vajrayana—leaning heavily on Tantra practices. They trace back to the different gurus, or lamas, who started the lineages.

THE NYINGMA TRADITION
(THE OLD ONES)

The Nyingma tradition of Tibetan Buddhism traces its roots back to Padmasambhava and is the oldest school of Tibetan Buddhism. Padmasambhava mixed native Bön practices and beliefs with Tantra Buddhism to develop a unique and mystical form of Tibetan Buddhism.

Guide to the Buddha's Teachings

Atisha wrote *Lamp for the Path of Enlightenment* for the Tibetan people, to answer the questions they had about practice and show them all the Buddha's teachings—distilled from sutras and tantras—in a short guide that simplified direction for practice. These teachings on the stages of the Path were known as *lam-rim. Lamp for the Path of Enlightenment* is still used in practice today.

It is believed that Padmasambhava found his disciples unready to experience the full disclosure of his knowledge, so he hid hundreds of teachings from them, to be revealed in the future to teachers more prepared for the knowledge he had to impart. Subsequently, teachers through the years have revealed these hidden treasures, known as *terma,* to their students to aid in their enlightenment.

There are nine paths to enlightenment in Nyingma, six based on the sutras, and three based on the tantras. Nyingma is based on the practice of Dzogchen—a practice of meditation that presupposes the existence of buddha-nature and strives to allow it to manifest.

Dzogchen has recently become very popular in the United States as a meditation practice.

THE BOUND BY COMMAND SCHOOL (THE KADAM)

The Bound by Command School traces its roots back to Atisha, a monk who taught in Tibet starting in 1040. Atisha was born Chandragarbha to a royal family in Bengal. He was renamed Atisha, which means "peace," by a Tibetan king.

Atisha brought to Tibet a synthesis of the three major vehicles of Buddhism. His coming initiated the era of the Second Transmission of Buddhism to Tibet, seminal for the Bound by Command School of Tibetan Buddhism but also for the Virtuous School and Transmitted Command School.

Atisha was also known as one of the living Buddhas among the Tibetan people. He promoted the premise that the teachings of the guru, the lama, should be held above all else as the lama can demonstrate the living nature of the teachings and directly shows the student how to practice. The teacher could choose the specific practices that would benefit the specific student.

The Bound by Command School of Tibetan Buddhism did not last long. It was considered too strict for the Tibetan people, prohibiting intoxicants, money handling, sexual relations, and travel.

THE SAKYA TRADITION

Founded in 1073 by Khön Könchok Gyelpo, the Sakya school took its name from the monastery of the same name in central Tibet. Sakya means "Gray Earth." The Sakya tradition, which developed out of the earlier Nyingma teachings, has been preserved to the present day through the unbroken succession of the heads of the Khön school. The lineage holders of the tradition pass down the transmission of the Path and Fruit (*Lam-dre*) teachings. The Path and Fruit teachings synthesize the teaching of the sutras and the tantras, and are designed to bring the student to enlightenment in a single lifetime.

The Sakya tradition continues to this day. The current head of the Sakya school is the forty-first in the lineage and practices in exile from Tibet.

THE KAGYU TRADITION (THE TRANSMITTED COMMAND SCHOOL)

The Transmitted Command School of Tibetan Buddhism can trace its roots back to two Indian masters: Naropa and Tilopa. These masters were skilled in advanced yogic practices. The emphasis in the Transmitted Command School has been and still is on practice and mysticism rather than academics. Kagyu tradition has some of the more familiar names in the history of Tibetan Buddhism. Naropa taught Marpa and Marpa took the teachings back to Tibet with him where he continued to practice as a layperson.

Marpa in turn passed the teachings on to his most famous student, Milarepa (1052–1135), one of the most popular figures of all time in Tibetan Buddhism. Milarepa started out as a dark figure in history—he was a black magician bent on revenging his widowed mother and sister who were being mistreated by relatives—but became a poet and a supremely powerful yogi who mastered self-knowledge and achieved liberation. He was legendary for his mystical powers.

Among Milarepa's disciples was Gampopa, who wrote *The Jewel Ornament of Liberation*. Gampopa received the Six Yogas of Naropa from Milarepa as well as the practice of Mahamudra ("Great Seal" and one of the most important practices in Vajrayana focused on realization of emptiness), and then combined them into one lineage—Dakpo Kagyu. The Dakpo Kagyu school then gave rise to four additional schools. One of the most successful of these schools, the Karma Kagyu school, is still going strong today and is passed down through the reincarnations of the Karma Kagyu teachers.

The Six Yogas of Naropa is one of the tantric practices unique to the Transmission Command School. It is a system of advanced tantric meditation passed down by Naropa that represents the completion stage teachings. Mahamudra practice is explained according to interpretations of sutra and tantra—with the goal being direct understanding of buddha-nature. Mahamudra was an effort to get back to the basics of meditation practice much like Chan did in China. Each of the schools within the Kagyu tradition approach Mahamudra differently.

THE GELUG TRADITION (THE VIRTUOUS SCHOOL)

The Virtuous School could be called the reform movement of Tibetan Buddhism. Started by Tsongkhapa in the fifteenth century, Gelug can be traced back to the Bound by Command School and was greatly influenced by the teachings of Atisha. Tsongkhapa reiterated the emphasis that Atisha had made on the monastic traditions and the importance of the guru. Tsongkhapa was extremely well educated in various schools of Buddhism and engaged in extensive meditation practices as well. The emphasis in the Gelug tradition is on monastic and academic study. Few masters, if any, are laypeople. Monks who train in the Gelug tradition receive advanced degrees in Buddhist philosophy and thought. These monks are known as *geshes*.

The Dalai Lamas come from the Virtuous School of Tibetan Buddhism and have been the spiritual and secular leaders of Tibet ever since. However, the Dalai Lamas are not the heads of the Virtuous School itself. The Dalai Lamas receive training in many if not all the Tibetan schools of Buddhism, and the leader of the Virtuous School is the abbot of the Ganden Monastery.

COMMON THREADS

All of the principal Tibetan traditions of Buddhism have more in common than not. The energy behind Tibetan Buddhism is the spirit of Avalokiteshvara ("Lord who looks down in compassion"), the bodhisattva of compassion. The Tibetans believe that anyone can attain enlightenment. The bedrock of Tibetan spiritual culture is the commitment that each individual makes to help all sentient beings toward enlightenment. These Vajrayana schools come from the Mahayana tradition and mix native and tantric elements into their practices.

The role of the guru (or lama) in Tibetan spirituality is key, especially when it comes to the more sophisticated tantric practices, for which a student needs attentive guidance. The mantra *Om mani padme hum* (Hail to the jewel in the lotus) is woven into the very fabric of their society. This mantra is ubiquitous. It is on the lips of all Tibetans, on the walls of buildings, on prayer flags, in art, in jewelry, in stonework, on prayer wheels. The mantra captures the spirit of Tibetan Buddhism.

Protector Against Peril

According to Buddhist scholar Michael Willis, Avalokiteshvara was invoked as a protector against the "Eight Great Perils" of the first millennium: shipwrecks, wrongful imprisonment, thieves, conflagrations, lions, poisonous snakes, wild elephants, and disease. Avalokiteshvara became the feminine Guanyin in China and Kannon in Japan. Avalokiteshvara is also known as Chenrezi in Tibet and remains male with his feminine aspects as Tara.

Tara

Tara is one of the important bodhisattvas in Tibetan Buddhism. She is the female embodiment of compassion (karuna) and loving-kindness (*maitri* in Sanskrit, *metta* in Pali). Atisha introduced the cult of Tara to Tibet in the eleventh century. According to myth, Tara was born from a lotus growing in a pool formed by tears of compassion shed by Avalokiteshvara when he saw the enormity of suffering that humanity experiences. Tara is also the mother of all buddhas. She also comes in different colors—green for divine energy and white for transcendent wisdom. In another myth, Amitabha Buddha radiated his thoughts into a lake where a lotus grew and later revealed Avalokiteshvara. He then changed himself into a monkey and mated with Tara to produce the ancestors of the Tibetan people.

THE DALAI LAMA

Bodhisattva of Compassion

The current Dalai Lama is regarded as the fourteenth incarnation of the bodhisattva of compassion, Avalokiteshvara. The original Dalai Lama came out of the Gelug or Virtuous School of Tibetan Buddhism. This third teacher in the Gelug lineage appeared as the incarnation of the compassionate bodhisattva and was subsequently named the Dalai Lama, or Ocean of Wisdom.

The current Dalai Lama was born on July 6, 1935, to a family of poor farmers in the province of Amdo in Tibet. His eldest brother, Thubten Jigme Norbu, had already been recognized as a reincarnation of a high lama (*tulku*), Taktser Rinpoche, so it was a surprise that another Rinpoche would be found within the family.

"For as long as space endures, and for as long as living beings remain, I, too, abide to dispel the misery of the world."

—The Dalai Lama

A tulku is a special lama, one who is reincarnated from a previous teacher. Since the Dalai Lama is the fourteenth in his lineage, he is a tulku. Thousands of tulkus have been recognized over the centuries and most of these have been men. The Dalia Lama has considered the idea that he will return as the fifteenth Dalia Lama in female form. The identification of a tulku was portrayed in the film *Kundun*, where monks disguised as peasants arrived at the future Dalia Lama's home when he was a child of three years old. The monks were following clues provided by the thirteenth Dalai Lama—dreams or information provided by oracles to find candidate children. Once children are identified they are examined for special marks or signs and their parents interviewed regarding their moral character. Finally, a test is provided where the young child must identify items that belonged to his predecessor, picking them out from similar items. If he can do this correctly, he will be designated a tulku. Stories abide about tulkus being able to remember details from their previous lives, including His Holiness the Dalai Lama. Tulkus are also known by the title *Rinpoche* ("Precious One"). The Dalai Lama is not only the reincarnated tulku of the Gelugpa clan and secular and religious leader of Tibet, he is also believed to be the reincarnation of Avalokiteshvara.

The thirteenth Dalai Lama had died in 1933, and while his body was in its period of sitting in state, his head mysteriously turned toward the area near Amdo—this was just one of the clues that sent the search party on its way.

Once the search party had narrowed down their focus, they found Tenzin Gyatso. The small boy is said to have immediately recognized one of the monks and when handed some items as a test he was able to pick out the ones belonging to the thirteenth Dalai Lama; he is said to have cried out, "It is mine!"

The three-year-old child was taken away from his family to be trained and prepared for his role as the fourteenth in the succession of Dalai Lamas. He was eventually reunited with his family and continued his intensive education and training. At the age of fifteen, with the Chinese invasion threatening the horizon, the Dalai Lama was formally made the leader of Tibet. The young leader tried to secure the assistance of Great Britain and America but was turned down. Tibet was going to have to face the might of the huge Chinese government alone. On March 17, 1958, the Dalai Lama consulted with the Nechung Oracle and was instructed to leave Tibet. For nine years, the Tibetan people had tried to hold back a full-scale invasion of the Chinese government, but in the winter of 1959, the Dalai Lama knew it was time to go. Disguised as a soldier, he slipped out of the country.

The first thirteen Dalai Lamas were:

1. Gedun Drub (1391–1474)
2. Gedun Gyatso (1475–1542)
3. Sonam Gyatso (1543–1588)
4. Yonten Gyatso (1589–1616)
5. Ngawang Lobsang Gyatso (1617–1682)
6. Tsang-yang Gyatso (1683–1706)
7. Kezang Gyatso (1708–1757)
8. Jampel Gyatso (1758–1804)
9. Luntok Gyatso (1806–1815)
10. Tshultrim Gyatso (1816–1837)
11. Khedrup Gyatso (1838–1856)
12. Trinley Gyatso (1856–1875)
13. Thubten Gyatso (1876–1933)

Tibetan Buddhism in different forms has found great popularity in the United States. There are monasteries and study centers for the various forms of Tibetan Buddhism all over the country. One of the most well-known teachers of Tibetan Buddhism to emigrate to the United States was Chögyam Trungpa.

He fled Tibet at the age of twenty in 1959. In 1970 he moved to the United States and established his first American meditation center.

He started Naropa University—the first Buddhist-inspired university in North America. There are more than one hundred Shambhala Meditation Centers throughout the world that were founded by Chögyam Trungpa. He was a prolific author, including the classic, *Cutting Through Spiritual Materialism,* and was responsible for bringing many teachers to the United States from Tibet. Although he died in 1987 at the age of forty-seven, he left a legacy of study and education that continues strongly to this day. The *Shambhala Sun* (now published as *Lion's Roar),* a bimonthly periodical, recently celebrated its thirtieth anniversary.

CHINESE BUDDHISM

Chan and Pure Land

As Chinese interest in Buddhism grew, a need for texts was established. Buddhism slowly took root in China as new texts were brought into the country and translated, thus becoming available to practitioners. By the seventh century, different schools of Buddhism arose in China. The two most prominent schools were the Chan and the Pure Land schools. Chan Buddhism would come to be known in the West and Japan as Zen Buddhism. Both Chan and Zen mean "meditation."

Bodhidharma Enters China

Early in the sixth century Emperor Wu of China was a devout student of Buddhism. He had built many temples, translated many sutras, and considered himself well versed in the teachings of the Buddha. When he heard that Bodhidharma, a renowned Buddhist monk, had arrived in China, he requested a meeting with the Indian monastic. In reference to the great works he had done in the service of Buddhism through the construction of monasteries and translation of core texts, Emperor Wu asked Bodhidharma, "What merit have I accumulated for all my good to Buddhism?"

"None," Bodhidharma replied.

Emperor Wu was shocked; this answer contradicted everything he thought he knew about Buddhism. It was a common belief that good deeds developed merit points. Giving food to a mendicant monk was considered good karma and insurance for a good rebirth, especially if the monk you gave to was a good student. Wu considered himself knowledgeable about Buddhism and wanted to engage Bodhidharma in conversation. He became defensive and decided to test the newcomer. "What is the meaning of enlightenment?" he asked.

"Vast emptiness, nothing sacred," Bodhidharma said.

This, too, must have confused the great emperor. This was not in line with his beliefs and he did not understand what it meant. Emperor Wu then asked in frustration, "*Who* are you?"

And Bodhidharma replied, "I don't know."

Emperor Wu still did not understand what Bodhidhama was telling him.

Shaolin Kung Fu

While Bodhidharma was at Shaolin Temple, he found the monks there to be in terrible physical condition. He helped them with their meditation practice and also helped them get back into top physical condition. It was here at Shaolin Temple that Shaolin Kung Fu was born.

Bodhidharma left the frustrated emperor and made his way up the mountains to Shaolin. It was here in a small cave that he meditated for nine years straight, facing a blank wall. Legend has it that he became frustrated with himself for falling asleep, so he cut off his eyelids to ensure he didn't fall asleep again. Artworks depicting Bodhidharma often show him with eyes wide open.

Bodhidharma, who personifies a serious commitment to meditation practice and the concept of emptiness, was the founder of Chan in China. The Chan school of Buddhism endeavored to keep Buddhism simple, and at its heart was the desire to get down to basics. It had few of the features of the Vajrayana school of meditation. Chan

Buddhism promotes the belief that meditation is the direct route to enlightenment—and with meditation buddha-nature is revealed.

Bodhidharma became the first Chinese patriarch, starting a transmission of Chan from one person to another, from mind to mind, until the present day, just as the Buddha passed the teachings so many years before.

CHINA: PURE LAND

The other main school of Buddhism to start in China around the same time was called Pure Land. This school of Buddhism, unlike Bodhidharma's Chan, did believe in a system of merits and also promoted the idea that there is more than one Buddha.

Adherents of this school also believe that this realm has many different fields, the best being that of paradise, or Pure Land.

A purified field surrounds buddhas and bodhisattvas. Out of their great compassion they create a space around them that is uncontaminated. This space is available for those who wish to join them. It is attributed to Amitabha Buddha (the Buddha of Infinite Light). Amitabha is known as Amituo Fo in China and Amida Butsu in Japan. The Pure Land is also known as Sukhavati ("Abode of Bliss")

Pure Land Buddhists believe in a paradise after death. Amitabha is host there. If you invoke the name of Amitabha (*Namo Amituo Fo*), you will be reborn into the Pure Land. Pure Land in your mind is the place where enlightenment takes place; it is not enlightenment itself.

Therefore, in Pure Land Buddhism, if you invoke the name of the Buddha you invoke the reality of Pure Land. This practice was less rigorous than the Chan practice and found widespread acceptability.

One could be reborn into a paradise here at any time. All you had to do was recite the Buddha's name over and over, and paradise was yours. There were no impediments to enlightenment once you attained Pure Land, so much of the work of practice was alleviated.

The Jingtu Lun is an important Pure Land text that outlines five forms of devotion:

- Expressing reverence for Amitabha Buddha
- Praising Amitabha's virtue by reciting his name
- Spoken aspirations to be born in the Pure Land
- Contemplation on the physical form of Amitabha, bodhisattvas who live in the Pure Land, and the Pure Land itself
- Transferring one's own merit to assist others in reaching the Pure Land

According to Buddhist scholar Michael Willis, "The Pure Land is described as a kind of paradise devoid of diversion, such as women and conflict, and superior to any heaven because Amituo resides there, prepared to preach the Dharma to all those who ask for assistance."

The Pure Land practice is comparable to the bodhisattva path, and its advocate Daochuo (562–645) argued that it would be more expedient in that degenerate age because Amitabha was there to help. The Pure Land path was easier too and therefore more accessible to common people.

Pure Land Buddhism is popular in the West today.

JAPAN

Fertile Territory

Toward the end of the twelfth century, Chan arrived in Japan and became "Zen." The samurai warrior spirit was thriving in Japan, and the rigors of Zen practice were welcomed by the Japanese. There are two classes of Zen that arose in Japan. The first was called Rinzai and was brought back from China by the Japanese monk Eisai. Eisai's student Dogen brought the second class of Zen to Japanese shores from China. This school of Zen was called the Soto school. We'll cover these two schools in much more detail in a chapter devoted to Zen Buddhism.

Both schools of Zen emphasized the importance of seated meditation. Over many years, the Soto school became larger than the Rinzai school in Japan (today, it might be as much as three times as large), though both schools are still very prominent. The strictness of practice in the monasteries historically inhibited many people from practicing Zen. But as Zen headed to the West in the twentieth century, this would no longer be the case.

NICHIREN BUDDHISM

Another Buddhist tradition arose in Japan in the early thirteenth century. A Buddhist monk named Nichiren was the founder of this school, which came to bear his name. Nichiren studied the Lotus Sutra and came to believe it was the embodiment of Truth. He believed that by reciting *Namu-myoho-renge-kyo* (Glory to the Lotus Sutra) one could evoke all the wisdom contained in its verses. The

Nichiren school has proliferated into many subschools. It remains popular today in Japan and the West and includes an evangelical branch that seeks converts. Much like the Hare Krishnas, someone from this tradition may approach you at an airport or on the street and encourage you to chant the mantra Namu-myoho-renge-kyo.

JAPANESE PURE LAND

The Pure Land practice went from China to Japan and was practiced from the aristocracy to peasants. One important text, written by Ojoyoshu, "Birth in the Land of Purity," helped to promote the popularity of these practices that emerged from the ninth to eleventh centuries. Honen (1133–1212) is considered the founder of the first Jodo (Pure Land) school in Japan. Honen gave up on getting to the Pure Land by personal effort. He forsook his monastic vows, took a wife, and substituted *tariki* (other power) for *jiriki* (self-power), feeling that this was more consistent with the Buddha's original teaching. He was discouraged that no buddhas had appeared since the time of Siddhartha. He saw Pure Land Buddhism as an alternative path and Amida Butsu as the key to everything. His followers founded Jodoshin ("True Pure Land School") that permitted its clergy to marry. The Jodoshin has persisted to contemporary times and remains the largest religious organization in Japan.

Honen's teachings created a paradigm shift for Buddhist practice, replacing the personal path of salvation with Amida, a universal savior who helped the faithful to reach his Pure Land. It was only in the Pure Land that one could achieve enlightenment. While initially suppressed, the Jodo school founded by Honen achieved great popularity and was the religion of the ruling class by the seventeenth century.

The Pure Land practices provided a "shortcut" through countless lifetimes to become a bodhisattva. It employs not only chanting but complex visualization of buddhas, bodhisattvas, and the Pure Land, especially Amitabha. The text "Visualizing the Buddha of Limitless Life Sutra" presents the story of Queen Vaidehi. The Buddha gave her a vision visible in a golden ray of light emanating from his forehead. In this vision she saw all the celestial worlds and chose her wish to be reborn with Amitabha. Buddhist scholar Michael Willis shares a segment of this text, "You should think of the *buddha* of Limitless Life. Why? Because the Body of the *buddha* is the Body of the Universe and it is within the mind of all beings. Therefore when you think of that *buddha* your mind becomes the One who has the thirty-two Magnificent Figures and the eighty Virtues. It is the mind that is to become a *buddha* and it is the mind that is the *buddha*. The Ocean of Omniscient Wisdom of all *buddhas* grows up from the mind."

What Percentage of the World's Population Is Buddhist?

Today it is estimated that approximately 9–10 percent of the world's population is Buddhist. Christianity weighs in with the largest percentage of adherents at 33 percent, and Islam comes in second at 18 percent. It is estimated there are 100 million followers of Theravada Buddhism worldwide; 360 million to 500 million followers of Mahayana; and 10 to 20 million Tibetan Buddhists.

It is not clear whether belief in the Pure Land is taken literally or metaphorically as purified states of mind. For indigenous Chinese and Japanese their relationship to Amitabha as savior is likely regarded as quite literal. In America, if you adopt these practices you have a choice. The Pure Land schools seem to move Buddhism from more of a rational psychology to a theistic, transcendent religion. The ease of these practices compared to arduous sitting meditation in Chan and Zen, and the promise (likely realized in bliss states as one chants the Amitabha mantras) of going to heaven increased its popularity in China and Japan. These practices resemble some of the Vedic practices that Siddhartha would have been familiar with in his search for the Way when he left the palace. Chanting the names of Shiva or Krishna, for example, was a common practice in pre-Buddhist India as it is today.

ZEN BUDDHISM

A New Interpretation of Buddha

The origins of Zen are found in China when Bodhidharma went there in the sixth century. In China it was called Chan, in Korea it was called Son, in Japan it was called Zen, all meaning "meditation."

Many Words, One Meaning

Zen is the transliteration of the Chinese word Chan, which itself is an abbreviation of channa, the transliteration of the Sanskrit dhyana (meditation).

Zen has had a large influence on Taiwan, Korea, Vietnam, Japan, and now the West, especially America, which is now the most vital center of Zen practice in the world. Zen, which emphasizes enlightened masters over scriptures and is the least academic of all the Buddhist schools, offers a fresh interpretation of the Buddha's teachings and forms of practice that are straightforward and profound.

ZEN PRACTICE, PRINCIPLES, AND HISTORY

Meditation is the core practice of Zen and teachers are notorious for irreverent, unpredictable, and unorthodox methods of teaching. For example, in one temple, the bell would ring after meditation and all the practitioners who had been in seated meditation for a long period of time would have to get up, legs still asleep, and run down the hall to the Zen master's chamber. Only those who showed up first would get an interview for that day. The novices stumbled over each other in this mad procession to get to the Zen master.

According to Professor Mark Blum, Zen is comprised of four principles:

1. Transmission outside the orthodox Buddhist teachers through its lineages
2. A belief that truth is not dependent upon established doctrine and a belief in the value of experience over the value of scripture
3. A direct point to the mind
4. An emphasis on examining one's original nature and the attainment of enlightenment

The Buddha's disciple Kashyapa (or Mahakashyapa) was the forebear of Zen. It was he alone who "got" the Buddha's teaching when he held up a flower and smiled. Seeing that flower occasioned Kashyapa's enlightenment, and his experience reflects the emphasis in Zen that transmission does not require language. Kashyapa was the first of twenty-eight Indian patriarchs culminating in Bodhidharma who went to China around 520 C.E. where he became the first Chinese patriarch of Chan. From China, Chan made its way to Vietnam in 580 C.E., and then to Japan and Korea around the twelfth century.

The Zen concept of sudden enlightenment led to the Southern school; whereas gradual enlightenment through long practice led to the Northern school. These historical schools correspond to Rinzai and Soto Zen, respectively. In Japan, the monk Eisai founded the Rinzai school and Dogen founded the Soto school. Eisai's monastery, Kenninji, is still active today.

Rinzai

Rinzai emphasizes sudden enlightenment that is predicated on everyone already having buddha-nature. The right context will bring this sudden realization of what is already there. This sudden burst of insight is called *kensho*. Koan practice (description to follow) is integral to the pursuit of sudden awakening (and so, too, might be the rationale for having the monks race to get an interview with the Zen master). The Rinzai school bristles against slow and silent illumination found in the Soto doctrine of *shikintaza* (just sitting). While the Rinzai and Soto schools disagree about meditation, both value meditation. In Rinzai you meditate not to attain wisdom but as an expression of wisdom. Wisdom is not confined to the cushion, and awakening can be found in the most mundane experiences of everyday life. Historically, Rinzai was practiced in urban centers by the elite shoguns and samurai, while Soto was more of a rural practice. As military culture declined in nineteenth-century Japan so did Rinzai.

"Body and mind of themselves will drop away and your original face will be manifested. If you want to attain suchness, you should practice suchness without delay."

—Dogen, on zazen practice

Seated Meditation

The practice of Rinzai *zazen* (seated meditation) employs the waking stick. If you slump during meditation or fall asleep, an attendant will strike you across your trapezius muscles with a wooden stick. The blow is designed not to harm but to wake you up to the task at hand—meditation. You can also request a blow if you feel your energy is flagging. Performed correctly, the blow will not injure.

Koans

Koans (anecdotes or riddles) are designed to short-circuit the rational mind and provide the basis for a sudden spiritual awakening. The most famous of these inscrutable puzzles is, "What is the sound of one hand?" As one Zen master said, "It is the place where truth is." Koans are an important part of Rinzai practice. Rinzai also emphasizes meetings with the master (*dokusan*) more so than Soto schools, as these meetings (whether one runs to the meeting or not) can also facilitate kensho. Students are normally assigned a koan in dokusan. As a Zen student you would try to answer the koan when you meet with the teacher. Answers are usually not verbal, but can be. They are not "yes/no," "this/that" answers. When you know the answer, you will know how to convey the answer to the teacher, and the teacher will recognize that the koan has been solved by the way you are in the interview. During your meditation practice you will reach a stage known as samadhi. Samadhi is a deep and focused meditation wherein concentration is effortless and complete absorption has been attained. Koan practice is done in the samadhi state.

ZAZEN

The Heart of Zen Practice

The heart of Zen practice is zazen. Zazen is seated meditation, and the total concentration of mind and body. Zazen can be described to you with words, but the words are not zazen and you will not have experienced zazen. You can study, discuss, and read about zazen but that is not zazen.

INSTRUCTIONS FOR ZEN MEDITATION

In Zen there tends to be a paucity of instruction for meditation technique. Rather, the emphasis is on the posture, but of course something else is always being added. Shunryu Suzuki, the famed Soto monk who helped bring Zen Buddhism to the United States, encouraged a very precise way of sitting that is dignified and stable. You would sit in the lotus or half-lotus posture with your back straight and your hands in your lap, left palm resting on your right palm with your thumbs touching and forming a bridge. This posture is dynamic and full of energy. In some Zen practices, you may be instructed to count your breaths, counting on each exhalation up to ten, and then back from ten to one.

Breathing

When beginning zazen you will pay careful attention to the breath. Now breathe in through your nose and out through your nose. Breathe from your diaphragm and feel it rise and fall with your breath. Let your breathing fall naturally, in and out, in and out. Now start to count your out breaths. Breathe in, breathe out, count "one." Breathe in, breathe out, count "two." Continue doing this until you get to ten and begin again. When you notice that you are no longer concentrating on the counting but instead your mind has started to wander to the future or the past, start counting at one again.

Acknowledge the thought and go back to the breath. In and out, one. In and out, two. Continue to do this until the bell rings. You will notice how hard it is to bring the mind back to the breath. The mind can be full of unruly monkeys jumping from tree to tree. Sitting practice helps you to train the monkeys, and eventually make them still.

Being Present

The practice of Zen is the practice of sitting. Just sitting with *nothing* else added. When nothing else is added you experience your enlightened nature. But most of the time the mind will be active with thoughts and images. It may get swept away by emotions and stories. Your job is not to get rid of thoughts but to come back. You are learning to be present in the moment.

Try to sit still. Do not move. This may seem impossible at first, but the more you move the more you will want to move. This will require working through discomfort and even pain. Zen is a harder path in this way because it has such a strong emphasis on form. You will learn a lot about yourself by doing so. Sometimes the physical pain can be quite powerful. Not all teachers are strict with posture and suggest moving rather than fighting through pain. But sometimes you'll be moving just out of habit. You will see how you wiggle around to get away from the moment. If you can, sit as still as a mountain. *Be* a mountain.

Beginner's Mind

As with all forms of Buddhism, the aim of Zen practice is enlightenment. Zen assumes that you are already enlightened. Enlightenment is not something you do or a destination you get to; it's already here. Zen is the here and now. *This* moment. This moment is just as it occurs; it is just as it is without adding anything to it. Zen is something you experience intuitively. It is not about your rational, intellectual thoughts. In fact, your rational, intellectual thoughts will only get in the way when it comes to Zen practice.

Tasting Enlightened Mind

Shunryu Suzuki, in *Zen Mind, Beginner's Mind*, says, "The beginner's mind knows many possibilities, the expert mind few." Having no preconceived notions, and the willingness to be open to new experiences, is the key to transformation. Having a taste of enlightened mind, you will recognize something you have always had, and somehow lost your connection to. Tasting enlightened mind is like going home.

You have, throughout your life, constructed an idea of who you are. Zen is being in the moment without the *I* construct, the *me* you have created for yourself. Zen exists in the moment with no thought, no ego, bringing nothing to the table. You achieve this realization of emptiness through zazen.

GROUP PRACTICE

The sangha is key to Zen practice. The sangha usually meets in the *zendo*, a large hall or room where zazen is practiced. When a group gets together to practice, certain rules must apply to ensure that order and the quality of practice is maintained. Each practice group might have its own rules of practice and there might be some variation. Some of the practices used by a sangha might include walking meditation, a dharma talk given by the teacher, tea service, sutra recitation, and bowing. Lighting of candles and incense might be part of the experience.

Teacher and Student

When the teacher gives a talk to the group it is called *teisho*. Teisho is not a lecture or a sermon. It is more of a presentation of insight to the students. Often the subject of a teisho will be a koan. A private encounter with the teacher is called dokusan. In dokusan the teacher will gauge the student's progress and do what is necessary to encourage the student to continue.

When the Student Is Ready

It is said that when the student is ready, the teacher appears. Although at the heart of Zen is the realization that you are already enlightened, the student–teacher relationship in Zen is a very important element of practice. A teacher will guide the student through the various stages of practice, helping the student toward enlightenment.

Zen is transmitted from person to person. A teacher will have become a teacher through direct transmission from his or her teacher. The teacher in Zen is called the roshi.

SESSHIN

A *sesshin* is a Zen meditation retreat. Sesshins vary greatly in length, from a weekend to several weeks or more. Zazen is usually practiced for ten or more hours a day, broken with *kinhin* (walking meditation), work practice, rest periods, teisho, and ritualized eating known as *oryoki*. The sesshin members rise before dawn and do zazen before breakfast, and they end the day with zazen. Dokusan is held anywhere from one to three times during the day.

Sesshins are periodic intensive practice sessions to augment daily practice. Sesshins are the optimum time to work on koan practice (Rinzai) or shikintaza (Soto), and the dokusan is most helpful and provides encouragement to a flagging spirit. Sesshins are extremely difficult and rewarding. They are wonderful opportunities for practice in a safe environment with no distraction except for your own monkey mind.

Opening the Gate

Chanting is an integral component to Zen practice, especially the Heart Sutra. It is woven into the ritual fabric of Zen practice. For instance a formal Zen practice period (in the Soto Zen tradition) will begin with a series of bows followed by the recitation of the Heart Sutra. An excerpt from the text can be translated as follows:

Avalokitesvara Bodhisattva practice deep Prajna *paramita* when perceive five *skandas* all empty, relieve every suffering. Sariputra, form not different from emptiness. Emptiness not different from form. Form is the emptiness. Emptiness is the form. Sensation, thought, active substance, consciousness, also like this. Sariptura, this is everything original character; not born, not annihilated not tainted, not pure, does not increase does not decrease. Therefore in emptiness no form, no sensation, thought, active substance, consciousness. No eye, ear, nose, tongue, body, mind; no color, sound, smell, taste, touch, object.

Once the chant is complete another series of bows are made. These prostrations while done in front of an image of the Buddha are not meant as idol worship. The Buddha sits as a symbol of human potential, your nature as an awakened being, and serves as a reminder of that possibility. The ritual of bowing and chanting creates a gate that the participants go through to mark the beginning of the formal practice period. Silence is maintained. Although the participants do not talk with one another, the practice of Zen is communal.

Walking Meditation

Walking meditation in Zen is called kinhin. Zazen is often broken up with a period or periods of kinhin to stretch the legs and give them some relief. The walking meditation is very slow and the steps are usually synchronized with the breath so that you step with the in-breath and step with the out-breath.

At the beginning of each sitting (that may last approximately forty-five minutes), each participant bows to the wall, turns 180 degrees clockwise, and waits until everyone in the room has done likewise. When everyone is standing ready to bow (hand in *gassho*— prayer position or Namaste), then everyone bows together, turns 180 degrees clockwise again, and sits down on their cushion. At the end of the sitting meditation period the bell rings and everyone arises from meditation, arranges their sitting space neatly, bows to the wall (Zen is practiced facing the wall), turns 180 degrees as before, waits for everyone to be ready to bow, and then the group bows together as one. A typical meditation period may last two and a half to three hours with alternating periods of sitting and walking (kinhin) and is followed by a group meal known as oryoki.

ZEN EATING

A Ritual of Awareness and Cooperation

At Shao Shan in East Calais, Vermont, the group in the zendo room may be approximately ten people. Once everyone has arrived, the group stands, places their hands in *gassho* (prayer position), and bows. Once seated, Japanese style, on the floor, the Zen master claps wooden sticks together to mark the start of the meal practice and there is another gassho. Now the food is served. At Shao Shan a simple meal is offered for lunch that consists of homemade squash soup, hummus, some greens, and steamed bread. The food service is an exercise in remaining attentive. Participants are required to pay keen attention to maintain the group harmony. The Zen master serves the soup from a large pot. The person farthest from her sits with hands in gassho, watching. When enough has been served, the hand is lifted toward the sky to signal "enough." That bowl is then passed back along the participants until it reaches that person, who sets it down. This process is repeated until everyone has soup. Then the hummus is passed around in a bowl. The people on one side of the table become the servers. You serve the person sitting across from you, who sits in gassho and raises one hand when enough has been served. You then serve yourself and pass the bowl to the person next to you. The bread is served in the same way. Once all the food has been served, the meal chant is recited in Japanese:

Hitatsu ni wa, ko no tasho o hakori, kano raisho o hakaru
Futatsu ni wa onore ga taku gyo no zen ketto nakatte k ni ozu
Mitsu ni wa, shin o fusegi toga o wanaruru koto wa tonto o Shu
to sa

Yatsu niw a, masa I ryo yaku o Kot to suru wa gyoko o ryozen ga Itatsu ni wa, jodo no tame no yue ni, ima Kono jiki o uku.

These five stanzas roughly translate to:

This meal is labor of countless beings, let us remember their toil.
Defilements are many, exertions few, do we deserve this offering?
Gluttony stems from greed, let us be moderate.
Our life is sustained by this offering, let us be grateful.
We take this food to attain the Buddha Way.

To recite the meal chant is to become intentional about eating. The goal is to be awake while food is consumed and to come out of the trance wherein eating is taken for granted. The first stanza reminds you that countless events took place to get this food to the table. It had to be prepared, bought, delivered to the store, planted in the ground, nurtured by rain, sun, and bacteria, and so forth. It is a reminder of the interconnected web of life and a reminder that events do not occur out of this interconnected context. This helps to foster appreciation for the unique gift this food represents. The second stanza asks you to reflect upon your efforts to date and to see where effort may be strong or needs improvement. The third stanza is self-explanatory, and at a deeper level resonates the Buddha's message of the Middle Way. Remember in his own path he experienced both extremes of indulgence and starvation. Moderation with food is a reminder to moderation in all things, avoiding extremes whenever possible. The fourth stanza reminds you that this food is vital to your survival, to nourish the body with nutrients. And the fifth stanza builds on the message of the fourth stanza and reminds you to put that nourishment to good use—to use it to work toward awakening.

Once the meal chant is recited and the reflections on its meaning made, there is one more step—the food offering. Everyone takes a small bit of bread and places it into a bowl. Later the group will go for a walk and offer this bread to the fish living in the pond near the zendo. Then eating begins!

Unlike vipassana meditation retreats where eating may be a very slow process, the group at Shao Shan eats at a relatively normal rate. However, one must be efficient and mindful of others while eating. Once the master has finished her portion, an offering of seconds is made. Everyone stops eating and the process of serving begins anew. Once everyone who wants seconds is served, another gassho is performed, and then everyone resumes eating. As with bowing before and after meditation, this is a group process and the meal does not end until everyone has finished eating. This communality is a natural deterrent to gluttony because no one wants to be the last one eating when everyone else is finished.

The meal ends with tea served as the hummus and bread were served; you serve the person across from you and then serve yourself. Then a serving tray is passed for the dishes and each of the participants wipes their portion of the table. Then gassho. Then standing. Then gassho. Lunch is now over. The entire process has been conducted in noble silence—when it goes smoothly no words or eye contact is exchanged.

Eating the meal in this ritualized way provides continuity to the practice, and it functions as a living reminder that all moments can be lived with intention. The entire Zen practice is an invitation to awaken. After lunch, a volunteer is solicited or someone is appointed the opportunity to do work practice by washing the dishes. Then a communal walk to make the food offering takes place. Then zazen practice resumes. This is a taste of the way of Zen.

TEA CEREMONIES

A Zen Ritual

Most Westerners think of tea as a breakfast drink or something to enjoy with toast at four o'clock in the afternoon. Most drink tea in a cup with a bag or an infuser and maybe a garnish of lemon and honey or a little bit of milk and sugar. In Zen Buddhism, tea is a ritual. Once you experience tea the Zen way, you will never look at a cup of tea quite the same way. Tea is ceremony itself.

"In the liquid amber within the ivory-porcelain, the initiated may touch the sweet reticence of Confucius, the piquancy of Lao-Tzu, and the ethereal aroma of Shakyamuni himself."

—Okakura Kakuzo, Japanese scholar

The tea ceremony is called *chanoyu*. It translates into "hot water for tea." Chanoyu is based on the principles of respect, harmony, purity, and tranquility. If you could bring these qualities into your everyday life, your life would be filled with utter peace. Everyone in the tearoom is equal, and great respect is paid to each person present. Everything in the tearoom matters, from the air you breathe to the flower arrangement to the actual space it is served in—everything contributes to the enjoyment of each moment of the tea ceremony.

The rules for the tea ceremony are to be followed exactly. Each moment matters and the sequence of events is laid out rigidly. The ceremony flows, and there is meaning in every gesture; each moment is to be savored. The tea ceremony is the way of life itself. It captures the essence of Zen—life in the moment with great attention.

In this regard, the tea ceremony is a mindfulness meditation. It is a moving meditation, practiced to cultivate samadhi. The repetition and rigidity of action allows you to enter a deep meditative state, as you know each movement coming your way. As you perform each part of the ceremony you do so with utter mindfulness, paying careful attention to each and every movement. When you whisk, you whisk. When you pour, you pour. When you drink, you drink.

In *The Book of Tea* by Okakura Kakuzo, the author tells us that there are actually schools of tea. These schools can be classified as Boiled Tea, Whipped Tea, and Steeped Tea. Practitioners in the West would fall into the latter category. Caked tea is boiled, powdered tea is whipped, and leaf tea is steeped.

VOCABULARY

First an introduction to the vocabulary of the tea ceremony. The tea ceremony takes place in the *chashitsu*—a room designed for the tea ceremony. This room is usually in the teahouse itself, which is usually within the gardens. Here are some other words you will want to familiarize yourself with:

- *Sayu*—hot water with which to make tea.
- *Furo*—brazier (a pan for holding hot or burning coals).
- *Chabana*—tea flower arrangement.
- *Fukusa*—a cleansing cloth, usually a square of silk, folded into a triangle, which hangs from the host's sash.
- *Kama*—a container for boiling water (kettle).

- *Kashi*—sweet candy snack.
- *Mizusashi*—container for cold water.
- *Chawan*—tea bowl.
- *Chakin*—napkin.
- *Chashaku*—scoop for tea.
- *Chaki*—tea container.
- *Kensui*—water waste container with *futaoki* (lid rest).
- *Hishaku*—water ladle.

In order to have a tea ceremony, you will also need the tea and charcoal for the fire.

Procedure

The guests are greeted by the host and ushered into the tearoom. The guests take their seats and the kashi is served and eaten. The kama has been set on the furo so that the water can boil. Then the host brings items necessary to start preparation of the tea. First he brings over the tea bowl containing the wiping napkin, the whisk, the tea scoop, and the container holding the tea. He then brings over the wastewater container, which holds the lid rest and the water ladle. The lid rest should be placed near the kettle with the water ladle on top of it. The lid rest is used to hold the lid of the kettle and is usually made of green bamboo. Now the host is ready to start preparations.

The host takes the fukusa and wipes the tea scoop and the tea container. This is done with intense concentration as the host's focus on meditation increases. This cleansing gesture signifies to the guests that everything is clean and the host cares about the purity of the service. Taking the ladle in hand, he scoops hot water out of the kettle and pours it into the tea bowl, and the whisk is then rinsed in the water. The water is then poured into the wastewater container, the bowl is cleaned with the wiping cloth, and the cloth is put back in its place. Now the tea can be made.

The tea used in the tea ceremony is powdered tea, so it has to be whipped. The host picks up the tea container in his left hand and the scoop in his right, and puts three scoops of tea into the tea bowl from the tea container. The water ladle is filled nearly to the brim with hot water, and enough water is added to the tea to make a paste. More water is added as necessary to get the correct consistency for the tea. The tea is briskly whisked, and then the host picks up the tea bowl and places it on top of his left palm. He holds the right side of the bowl with his right hand, then turns it twice away from himself, a full turn of the wrist each time, so that the front of the bowl is facing away from the host. Then the tea bowl is placed in front of the guests, and the first guest picks up the bowl and holds it the same way.

Origins of the Ceremony

The tea ceremony traces its origins to the fifteenth century and conversations between Zen monks and the nobility. The goal is to combine aesthetics with meditative calm. The monk Shuko formulated the four principles. Sen no Rikyu changed the chanoyu from opulence to elegant simplicity in the sixteenth century. The door to the newly designed chashitsu was so low that participants had to bow on their way in. Samurai were asked to leave their swords outside. The interior was blank with the exception of a single piece of art.

The first guest to pick up the bowl will turn to the next guest, *gassho,* and offer the tea bowl. The guest will bow back and decline. Then she will gassho to the host, pick up the bowl, and hold it in the same way. She raises it a little bit while bowing again to show gratitude, then turns the bowl toward herself. She then drinks from the side of the bowl.

She wipes off the bowl with her thumb and finger and then turns the bowl back to the front. She admires the craftsmanship of the bowl—tea bowls are a work of art and the choosing of the tea bowl is part of the beauty of the ceremony—and returns the bowl to the host, turning it so the front of the bowl faces the host. Before she returns the bowl, she can ask questions about the bowl, such as "Where was this bowl made?" and "Does this bowl have a name?" The host pours water into the tea bowl, swirling it around to cleanse the bowl, then pours the water into the wastewater container.

The process is repeated for the next guest. When the last guest has had tea, the host cleans the tea bowl with the cold water and reverses the process. In the winter and spring months, a *ro* (a sunken hearth) is used instead of the furo, which is used the rest of the year so that the tearoom does not get uncomfortably hot.

WHY MEDITATE?

An Essential Part of Buddhism

Meditation is an elemental part of Buddhism. Even though the various schools of Buddhism approach meditation differently, mindfulness is a common core. For Westerners, meditation is one of the key attractive features of Buddhism, providing a methodology for transformation. Meditation provides an antidote to problems of self that Westerners find so vexing. Buddhism also provides a philosophical system that speaks to many people who want to live a life less ruled by greed, hatred, and delusion.

WHY MEDITATE?

Meditation can transform your life. It can change your brain and it can reduce stress and anxiety, help you to sleep better, energize you, make you more patient, get you in touch with how you feel both emotionally and physically, provide a quiet space in your day, and much more.

According to the meditation teacher Shinzen Young, mindfulness meditation provides three benefits:

- Sensory clarity
- Concentration
- Equanimity

Twenty minutes a day can change your life. If meditation improves sensory clarity, and if your experiences are twenty percent richer than they were before meditation, then the twenty minutes per day you spend meditating increases how much life you experience. What if meditation made things twice as rich? You can do the math! Improved concentration is another benefit of meditation. Can you use more concentration in your life? Would your work performance improve? Your relationships? Your golf game? Equanimity is the ability to handle any situation with a matter-of-fact and engaged attention. It is the ability to be calm during a storm. Meditation helps to cultivate equanimity along with sensory clarity and concentration.

MEDITATION GEAR

Of course you don't need any supplies to meditate, but traditionally many Buddhists have used things to accompany their meditation routines, from altars and incense, to cushions and bells. Here are some supplies you might want to consider:

- A meditation cushion (*zafu*)
- A cushion to put your meditation cushion upon (*zabuton*)
- Incense
- Timer, bell, or Tibetan singing bowl
- Altar
- Altar cloth
- Candles
- Flowers
- Devotional objects such as a statue of the Buddha
- Prayer beads

Buddhists call their meditation cushions zafus. Zen practitioners traditionally have round zafus and Tibetan practitioners usually have square zafus. The zafu can be placed on a zabuton, which is a large, flat, square cushion that protects the knees from the floor.

Traditionally, incense is burned for the duration of the meditation. Incense can be used as a timer for meditation sessions. Once the incense is burned, the time is up. This could be one of the original uses for incense. Incense also covered unpleasant body odors that may have arisen during meditation sessions, and helped keep flies out of the zendo. An altar is used for several reasons. First, repetition, habit, and ceremony play a large part in meditation practice. The altar is a visual reminder of the importance of practice. It is an indicator of your commitment to practice. And an altar sets the stage for energizing the senses: Gazing at the Buddha, smelling the incense, and bowing or doing prostrations all combine to form a context for the practice itself.

"I practice meditation
To subdue the dragon of desire."
—Wang Wei, eighth-century poet

If possible, it is a good idea to have the altar in a room or part of a room you will not use for any other purpose. If not possible, the altar can be in a corner of a room that can be accessed for practice. If you choose to have an altar, make it your own. You might find altars configured in the following way. A Buddha statue is placed in the center of the altar to focus attention on the two jewels of the Buddha and the dharma. Implements (such as bells or a vajra) are placed to the side of the Buddha. The incense and incense holder are placed in the center of the altar. You can put incense in an incense holder or fill a small bowl with rice to hold the incense stick. Flowers can be placed on the altar to symbolize the nature of impermanence. A candle can also be placed to one side. The candle symbolizes the light of truth brightening the darkness of delusion.

A timer or Tibetan singing bowl would stay by your zafu and zabuton and would be struck to begin and end the meditation sessions. You can follow the sound of the bell with your mind and start your meditation.

Singing Bowls

Tibetan singing bowls traditionally come with a striker and a silk-covered cushion to rest the bowl on. They come in a variety of sizes from quite small to large. You can use a Tibetan singing bowl to mark time, as an alarm or a timer, or to hold your incense sticks.

Prayer beads and devotional objects can be placed on the altar. Prayer beads are held during Tibetan-style meditation. Prayer beads traditionally came from the wood of the Bodhi Tree. A typical strand of prayer beads has 108 beads. Like a rosary, these prayer beads are used in the practice of *japa*, repeating a mantra such as *Om mani padme hum*. The beads are used to keep track of the number of repetitions. Different schools of Buddhism use different meditation items.

POSTURE

In virtually all Buddhist meditations, you are required to take a specific posture. Put on some comfortable clothing and take off your shoes. Sit with your legs crossed, in lotus (legs crossed with each foot on the opposite thigh), or half-lotus (one foot on the opposite thigh and the other foot folded on the floor) position if you can. Put the zafu underneath you and sit forward on it so that your knees are touching the ground. You can also put the cushion between your legs and kneel with most of your weight resting on the cushion so your legs don't fall asleep. This is called sitting *seiza*. You can also sit Burmese-style (both legs folded and flat on the floor with either the right or left foot forward), or seated in a chair with back straight and feet firmly on the floor. If your knees do not reach the floor, you may want to place a towel or another cushion underneath to support them. Make sure you are in a quiet space with no distractions such as televisions, radio, or other people who are not practicing.

Keep your spine as straight as possible and the top of your head pointed toward the ceiling. Rest your hands in your lap, palms up, with one hand cradling the other. Touch your thumbs gently together. You can also rest your hands palms up or palms down on your thighs. Your lips touch lightly and your tongue can gently touch the roof of your mouth. Make sure you are not holding tension in your shoulders or anywhere else. Your eyes can be open or closed. If open, try to relax them and loosen their focus.

Set a time limit for your meditation and use a bell, timer, or incense to indicate when time is up. You can start with very short periods, such as ten minutes, building up to longer periods of sitting as you continue practicing.

When your timer goes off or your sitting time is over, be careful that you do not jump to stand up. Often your legs can go to sleep, and if you stand up quickly you might fall over. Take your time, shake out your legs, and then stand slowly. You may want to bow to honor the practice you just completed.

It may help to do light stretching before getting into your meditation position. If you go to a practice center you will get further instructions.

THE BREATH

Awareness of breathing is fundamental to Buddhist-style meditation. The breath is your constant companion. If you're not aware of your breathing, then becoming enlightened is not going to be your top priority. Breathing is also happening now, and it will help to bring you into the present moment and into your body as it is now. You will taste the sense of being a living, breathing human being (rather than human "doing," which you are most of the time). Every breath you take is colored by your emotional experience, and so familiarizing yourself with the process of breathing helps you to monitor your emotional state and to intervene early if anxiety or other distressing emotions arise. When you breathe, allow the process to be natural. Don't try to breathe a "meditative" breath. You will probably find that your breathing will slow on its own, and that is fine. If it doesn't that is also fine. Just notice the breathing that is happening now.

SHAMATHA AND VIPASSANA

Forms of Meditation

There are different techniques for meditation. Zazen, or Zen meditation, was covered in a previous chapter. Two other types of meditation are *shamatha* meditation and vipassana meditation. Shamatha means "calm abiding" or "dwelling in tranquility" and vipassana means "insight." Vipassana is also called "insight meditation." Most Buddhist traditions employ these as central practices (that is, Theravada) or as component practices (for example, Tibetan).

Ways of Breathing

The *Sathipathana Sutta* provides very detailed instructions on breathing meditation with sixteen different ways to attend to breathing. These myriad ways of attending to breathing are outlined in Larry Rosenberg's book, *Breath by Breath: The Liberating Practice of Insight Meditation*.

SHAMATHA MEDITATION

Shamatha meditation techniques involve concentration on one thing, whether it is your breath or the sound of rain. "Calm abiding" means sitting with one's breath, or other point of concentration, gently coming back to this point whenever attention wanders. Concentration is the foundation for later insight practices and is not the final goal.

The benefits of one-pointed concentration are many. You can make great progress in any undertaking you choose if you can focus diligently on the task at hand. Shamatha meditation invites you to focus on one point calmly and quietly without undue exertion. The quality of this concentration is firm but not forced. Think of holding a bird in your hand. If you hold it too loosely, it will fly away. If you hold it too tight, you will crush it. Pursue concentration along the Middle Way, with effort, zeal, and interest.

VIPASSANA MEDITATION

As compared to one-pointed concentration, vipassana meditation—insight meditation—is a more open awareness. Attention is directed to whatever arises in the field of experience. In the Burmese tradition the field of awareness is limited to the body; and in the Thai tradition, for example, the field of awareness is open to any mental content including thoughts, images, feelings, sights, and sounds, in addition to bodily sensations. Attention to the arising and fading away of bodily sensations or other experiences will show you impermanence in action. It will show you how these experiences are "empty" of any underlying substantial reality. You will experience yourself in a dramatic new way.

Shamatha is the foundation for vipassana meditation. Once your mind is still and calm, you will have the ability to watch whatever arises in your mind. Once the mind is quiet, you can notice when it wanders off. If your mind is perfectly still, you can abide with your breath. If your mind wanders off, just observe where it goes. When you catch your mind wandering away, you can do one of two things. The instructions will vary according to your teacher's tradition.

One approach is simply to come back to whatever is happening in the body and move away from the story of the thoughts to the recognition that thoughts are happening. Another approach is to give the mental content a label. This practice is called mental noting. So if thoughts arise, note "thoughts" or "thinking." You just stick a label on it and move on to the next moment. Mental noting helps you to be objective with your experience and avoid self-judgment. If you notice judgment is active, such as when you are criticizing yourself for attention wandering, note this "judgment" and move your attention from the judgment to the next breath.

OTHER FORMS OF MEDITATION

Shamatha and vipassana are the basic Buddhist meditation practices. Vipassana can also be taken "on the road" in the form of walking meditation. There are also other practices based on the Four Immeasurables, such as lovingkindness and compassion, and other meditative techniques such as visualization, mantras, and chanting.

Lovingkindness (Metta) Meditation

Compassion, generosity, open-heartedness, and lovingkindness are all wonderful qualities to acquire. They are what the Buddha called the Four Immeasurables or the Limitless Abodes. What is lovingkindness, or as it is sometimes translated, loving friendliness? Metta practice is a curious hybrid of Buddhist and yoga practices. Instead of just working with whatever arises as you would in vipassana, you intentionally direct your attention to the generation of loving feelings. To do this you may recall someone who is very dear to you, someone whom you can readily access loving feelings. You can feel how this suffuses your heart with love and a sense of openness. Depending on the specific teacher you will direct that loving feeling in various ways. There are some commonalities. You direct that loving feeling to others and yourself, and you do so with four specific intentions:

- May you be free from danger; May you be safe.
- May you have happiness; May you have peace.
- May you have physical well-being and health; May you be free from illness.
- May you have ease of well-being; May you be free from unnecessary struggle and pain.

The secret is that this is really good for you. Staying in a state of unforgiveness toward people and situations leads to elevated stress levels and can damage your health. You can expand the circle of metta further to your sangha, your community, your country, the world, and all sentient beings.

Fighting the Trance of Unworthiness

Tara Brach teaches a form of metta meditation that speaks to the "trance of unworthiness" that afflicts so many in the West. This lack of self-acceptance is humorously and compassionately explored in her bestselling book, *Radical Acceptance: Embracing Your Life with the Heart of a Buddha*. She is the founder and senior teacher of the Insight Meditation Community of Washington.

Another meditation that focuses on compassion is called *tonglen*—sending and receiving. Pema Chödrön writes about tonglen in *When Things Fall Apart*. Tonglen, she says, is "designed to awaken bodhicitta, to put us in touch with genuine noble heart. It is the practice of taking in pain and sending out pleasure and therefore completely turns around our well-established habit of doing just the opposite." The way to practice tonglen is to breathe in suffering—your own suffering, the suffering of others, those with disease, with heartache, with pain—and breathe out wellness and kindness and direct it toward others, toward yourself. Breathe in pain, breathe out healing. Breathe in hatred, breathe out love. In this manner you cultivate bodhicitta and awaken a compassionate spirit inside yourself.

MANTRA MEDITATION

Mantras are often used as meditation devices by Buddhists. A mantra is basically a sound vibration. A constant repetition of a mantra (whether silent or aloud) can help to clear the mind of debris. Distractions fall away as the mind focuses on the repetitive sound. You can use a specific mantra for a specific spiritual purpose or you can use the mantra in a general way for focusing the attention and clearing the mind.

Different vehicles of Buddhism tend to use different mantras.

MANTRAS		
Pure Land	Tibetan	Nichiren
Namo Amito	Om mani padme hum	Namu myoho renge kyo
Glory to Amitabha	Hail to the jewel in the lotus	Glory to the Lotus Sutra

For example, according to Gen Rinpoche, the venerated Buddhist teacher, *Om mani padme hum* is associated with Avalokiteshvara, the bodhisattva of compassion. This mantra has six syllables. Each of the six syllables is said to aid you in the perfection of the six *paramitas* of the bodhisattvas. The six paramitas are generosity, ethics, patience, perseverance, concentration, and wisdom. Chanting the mantra *Om mani padme hum* will help you master these six perfections, and mastering these six perfections will help you to become a bodhisattva.

Mind Deliverance

The word *mantra* is actually Sanskrit for two words: "man" and "tra." *Man* can be translated as "mind" and *tra* can be translated as "deliverance."

CHANTING, VISUALIZATION, AND WALKING

Supportive Practices

The Buddha discouraged attachment to rites and rituals. Neverthe-less, all the Buddhist traditions engage chanting of liturgical texts. To chant the texts is to concentrate the mind and to send a powerful vibration into the atmosphere surrounding you. Chanting in a group can be a very powerful experience. In Tibetan Vajrayana practices, chanting rituals can last for hours. Traditional Buddhists will chant mantras and sutras for the accumulation of merit.

The Triple Refuge chant is popular in many traditions. You recite the phrase, "I take refuge in the Buddha, I take refuge in the dharma, I take refuge in the sangha" three times.

Buddham saranam gacchami
Dhammam saranam gacchami
Sangham saranam gacchami
Dutiyampi Buddham saranam gacchami
Dutiyampi Dhammam saranam gacchami
Dutiyampi Sangham saranam gacchami
Tatiyampi Buddham saranam gacchami
Tatiyampi Dhammam saranam gacchami
Tatiyampi Sangham saranam gacchami

Many believe that chanting sacred texts can help to secure a favorable rebirth, and families with this belief will enjoin a Buddhist monk to recite sutras at the time of death. These texts will be heard by the deceased in the *bardo* state. The monk will chant from the classic text the *Bardo Thodol* (the *Liberation Through Hearing in the Intermediate State* and popularly known as the *Tibetan Book of the Dead*). The bardo is an intermediate state, a way station of sorts, which will determine the place of the dead person's rebirth. What happens during this forty-nine-day period is believed to be crucial for the next rebirth. So, too, the moment of death is crucial for what comes next, so the Tibetans undergo a great deal of preparation for this moment, and they use the *Bardo Thodol* and practices such as powa (transference of consciousnddess) to aid them.

VISUALIZATION

Visualization is a key practice in Vajrayana (Tibetan Buddhism). In visualization practice you would select an object to visualize such as the Buddha, bodhisattva, mandala, or other sacred object, and then you would concentrate on that object in the image space of your mind (that is the mental screen that appears around your forehead). Rather than letting the imagination run wild into future and past scenarios, it is recruited to aid practice. Visualization can help you to achieve mindfulness and spiritual empowerment by taking on the qualities of the imagined deities, changing habit patterns of mind, and so forth.

Visualization was practiced in China in the late fourth and early fifth centuries. Here practitioners would meditate on images such as the "Medicine King." Visual contemplation of Amitabha Buddha became a central component of Pure Land Buddhism in sixth-century Chinese Buddhism. These practices had many forms. To visualize the Buddha in your mind is to make your mind Buddha.

WALKING MEDITATION

Walking meditation is a wonderful complement to seated meditation, mindfulness, or mantra practice. Walking meditation is a way to practice mindfulness while moving around the world you inhabit. If you leave your meditation on the floor with your zafu, you won't make as much progress as you will if you take it with you into your day.

Because walking meditation proved so beneficial, the Buddha and his disciples used it in their practice. In Thailand walking meditation is such a fundamental part of practice that a walk is built into each meditation center for the monks' use. There are obvious physical benefits to walking meditation as well. Even slow walking provides stretching and a respite from the strenuousness of prolonged seated practice. Walking meditation can rejuvenate the mind and the body. Walking aids concentration, digestion, promotes physical fitness, and rejuvenates the body—and it can be done while practicing mindfulness.

PILGRIMAGE

Traveling to Sacred Sites

On his deathbed, the Buddha instructed his followers to visit the important sites from his life—the places of his birth, enlightenment, first sermon, and death—because these would inspire powerful emotions and propel their practice.

The dissemination of the Buddha's remains and other relics expanded this "sacred geography." Subsequently, mountains became sacred pilgrimage sites. These sites include Mount Kailash in Tibet, Mount Fuji in Japan, Mount Wutai in China, and Adam's Peak in Sri Lanka. Tibetan pilgrims may circumambulate long distances making full-body prostrations. Some of these journeys may be hundreds of miles long and take years to complete, one prostration at a time. To protect themselves, the pilgrims wear leather aprons and hand and knee protectors. Pilgrimage is a special form of practice, away from daily routines; the pilgrim brings the intention of devotion to the journey.

"These, Ananda, are the places that a devout person should visit and look upon with feelings of reverence. And truly there will come to these places, Ananda, devoted monks and nuns, laymen and laywomen, reflecting: 'Here the Tathagata was born! Here the Tathagata became fully enlightened in unsurpassed, supreme Enlightenment!'"

—The Buddha

Certainly, the Buddha spent a lot of time walking around northern India with his retinue of followers. Walking meditation is an important practice for mindfulness. You can embody this spirit each time you walk in a deliberate manner. As a lay practitioner you may not have the time to walk the equivalent of a marathon, but as the Vietnamese Buddhist spiritual leader Thich Nhat Hanh said, peace can be in every step.

A pilgrimage is much more than a holiday with a spiritual destination. A pilgrimage is a journey to a shrine or sacred place that can change the traveler in an irrevocable way. The Buddha made pilgrimages all over India, traveling from place to place, spreading his teachings. Today you can walk in the Buddha's footsteps and follow his path. If you are interested in experiencing some of the sacred places in the history of Buddhism, you will have many to choose from.

The four holy sites of Buddhism are: Lumbini, the Buddha's birthplace; Bodh Gaya, the site of enlightenment; Sarnath, the site of the First Sermon; and Kushinagara, where Buddha reached paranirvana. This list is not comprehensive. You can also visit Sri Lanka, Myanmar, Bhutan, China, Taiwan, Tibet, Thailand, Vietnam, Japan, Korea, and more. The Buddha himself may not have left footsteps in these countries, but Buddhist culture and history is rich and there are many wonderful places to experience.

NEPAL

The Buddha was born in Lumbini in what is now Nepal. Places of interest to visit in Lumbini include Lumbini Garden, which contains the Ashokan Pillar and the image of Queen Maya (Maya Devi); Puskarni, the sacred pool; Sanctum-Sanctorum of the Birthplace; and the Buddhist Temple. The Ashokan Pillar was erected by King Ashoka in homage to the Buddha and contains an inscription dedicating the site to the Shakyamuni. The image of Maya Devi is inscribed into a pagoda-like structure. The image itself is in bas-relief and pictures Maya holding on to the baby Buddha who is standing on a lotus petal. Puskarni is the sacred pool in which it is said that Maya bathed the baby Siddhartha soon after he was born. Sanctum-Sanctorum is the holiest of places in the garden—within the Sanctum-Sanctorum is a stone slab that marks the exact spot the Buddha was born. Also of interest is the nearby Buddhist Temple. And not too far from Lumbini is Kapilavastu, where Siddhartha's father, Suddhodhana had his palace.

INDIA

Bodh Gaya is, perhaps, the most important of the pilgrimage sites, the place where Siddhartha attained awakening under the pipal tree. This Bodhi Tree (tree of awakening) is believed to be the ancestor of the tree that currently grows in Bodh Gaya next to the great stupa at the Mahabodhi Temple. Cuttings from the original tree have been planted around the Buddhist world and temples erected next to them.

Ashoka set up the first building in Bodh Gaya in the third century B.C.E. The current Mahabodhi Temple was built in the sixth century on the orders of the Sri Lankan monk, Mahanama. Today, the temple has been restored and is a great icon of Buddhist devotion. For example, in 1985, His Holiness the Dalai Lama came to Bodh Gaya to give the Kalachakra Tantra ceremony. Two hundred and fifty thousand Tibetans descended upon this tiny village to participate in this ritual, many of them in exile and others receiving special permission from the Chinese government to attend.

Among them were 10,000 Tibetan Buddhist monks and approximately 1,000 Westerners. This was the Kalachakra Tantra's largest audience to date. The Dalai Lama chose this spot as the most auspicious to offer these teachings, including teachings from Santideva's *Guide to the Bodhisattva's Way of Life*. Everyone in attendance took the bodhisattva vows from His Holiness. The place of Siddhartha's enlightenment is known as the *vajrasana* ("diamond throne").

You can also see a cave where Siddhartha practiced asceticism and the village of Uruvela, where the young Siddhartha broke his fast after attaining enlightenment.

Sarnath, several miles from Varanasi, is another major pilgrimage site where the Buddha gave his First Sermon in the deer park and started the Dharma Wheel turning. Sites of interest in Sarnath include Ashoka's Pillar (which used to have the Lion Capital on top of it, but now it resides in the Sarnath Museum), the ruins of the Mulagandhakuti, and the enormous Dharmek Stupa—a tower that dates back to the fifth or sixth century.

To the east is the modern Mulagandhakuti Vihara, which is said to house the original relics of the Buddha in a silver casket. The casket was recovered from the ruins of the first-century temple. The temple has beautifully painted walls that depict the Buddha's life story. The Sarnath Museum contains some of the greatest treasures of Indian Buddhist art. There is also an archaeological museum and the remains of a monastery from the third century B.C.E.

Also of interest in India is Rajgir, the home of Vulture Peak, site of many of the Buddha's teachings.

Kushinagara is the site of the Buddha's death. It is here in the sala grove that he reached paranirvana and passed into death. Places of interest in Kushinagara include the Nirvana Stupa, built over the spot where the Buddha died; the Makutabandhana Stupa, which marks the place of the Buddha's cremation; and a large stone reclining Buddha, housed in the Nirvana Temple.

GROWING UP BUDDHIST

Practicing Buddhism in the Family

Babies are not born Buddhist. Parents train their children in the dharma, teaching them the skills of meditation and mindfulness, the ethical precepts, moral codes, and rituals. The children will take refuge in the Three Jewels if and when they decide to do so. There is no passing of the religion through the parents to the children, as in some of the other great religions of the world.

There is no baptism or naming ceremony, no monastic intervention in the birth of the baby whatsoever. Family is very important in Buddhist life but there is no central Buddhist office, church, or higher authority, and Buddhism does not have much to do with family ritual. Families are largely a secular matter and not a matter of monastic relevance. Everything falls to the individual, and each person's enlightenment is his or her own responsibility. But Buddhism nonetheless infiltrates the daily life and spirit of the Buddhist family as the family practices together.

How Old Should a Child Be When Starting a Meditation Practice?

Young children have trouble sitting still. Forcing them to sit still for long periods of time is probably an exercise in futility or an unnecessary punishment. However, innovative practitioners are finding ways to engage children of all ages in mindfulness practice through music, games, and altering the instructions of an activity, such as focusing on the soles of their feet when they walk. Teens and young adults can do seated practice and many retreats are available for these kids. The Insight Meditation Society and other retreat centers offer family retreats.

As Buddhism moved to the West the problem of how to simultaneously maintain a meditation practice and raise a family became a pressing issue. Where could parents find the time to dedicate to their practice if they had young children to care for? As James William Coleman tells us in *The New Buddhism*, Western Buddhist centers have not done a satisfactory job of providing for children so that their parents can practice. Some have offered limited childcare to encourage parents to practice, but even those are few and far between.

Parents have come up with creative solutions, such as sharing childcare time with other families who practice. But as Buddhism moves away from monastic focus and laypeople get more involved with Buddhist monasteries and centers, a solution will have to emerge that frees up parents to practice while their children are well cared for.

RITES OF PASSAGE

All spiritual traditions have their rites of passages. Buddhism is no exception in this respect, but traditions vary from school to school and country to country.

In Thailand and Myanmar young men become monks in a rite of passage and live a monastic life for at least three months, while Tibetan children are given a herd of yaks to take care of. In the West, programs are being developed for children as Buddhism comes of age in this part of the world and children become an active part of the Buddhist community.

WOMEN IN BUDDHISM

A Slow Acceptance

Like most of recorded history, the early years of Buddhism report few stories of women. The Buddha's mother is mentioned, but she died soon after Siddhartha was born. He was then raised by his aunt, his mother's sister, Prajapati. In fact, it was Prajapati who, after the Buddha's enlightenment, went to him and asked if women could also join the sangha. She was refused but she persisted, asking a second time, and then a third. But the Buddha was unmovable and denied his good aunt's request.

Prajapati cut off her hair and donned the yellow robes of the mendicant monks. She followed the Buddha and pleaded with him to allow women to become members of the sangha.

The Story of Two Monks

There is the traditional story of two monks who are walking down the road. They come to a small stream and there is a frail woman waiting at the water's edge. One monk offers to carry the woman across the water, and he does so and puts her down on the other side of the stream. The monks walk on for miles and the other monk says, "I can't believe you touched that woman; it is forbidden." The monk laughed and said, "I put her down miles ago. Why are you still carrying her?"

It wasn't until Ananda interfered on Prajapati's behalf that the Buddha finally relented. The Buddha believed women were equal to men with regards to the ability to attain enlightenment, but practical matters, such as not offending the sangha's wealthy patrons, kept him from agreeing that it was a good idea to allow women into the community. However, he did finally say yes, and women were subsequently permitted to give up their worldly lives and enter as members of the sangha. Five hundred women joined Prajapati, including Yasodhara, the Buddha's abandoned wife. However, the women were given eight rules they had to follow that separated them from the monks and made them subordinate to their male counterparts. Buddhist monks and nuns are segregated in Asia and are discouraged from having physical contact.

The Mahayana texts support the Buddha's statement that men and women were equally equipped for enlightenment, and most traditions in Buddhism have included nuns (bhikkunis). But Buddhist literature portrays the difficulties the men had with accepting the women as part of monastic life. Women were portrayed as seductresses and unclean creatures—most likely due to men's unfulfilled sexual drives and their inability to stave off lust and desire.

Indeed, women struggled in Buddhism as they have struggled in most other religions. For many years, and in many traditions in Buddhist history, women were proclaimed to be equal in theory but were in fact subordinate in practice. For example, in 1979, Irish-American Maura "Soshin" O'Halloran wrote home to America to tell her family that she was the first woman ever admitted to Toshoji Temple in Japan.

In the West today a great percentage of the teachers of Buddhism are women. Teachers such as Pema Chödrön, Tara Brach, Charlotte Joko Beck, Sharon Salzberg, Silvia Boorstein, Joanna Macy, Narayan Liebenson, Grace Schireson, and many others have strengthened the dharma with their wise teaching.

In *Zen Women: Beyond Tea Ladies, Iron Maidens and Macho Masters*, Grace Schireson tells the untold story of women in Zen. The unfortunate truth is that the history of Buddhism is not one of gender equality. While the Buddha did finally relent after persistent pressure from his aunt Prajapati to admit women into the sangha against the norms of the time, admittance has not translated to equivalence of opportunity. She tells the story of a male Zen master who responded to a female student's question, "How many women teachers were at the conference (a North American Zen conference)?" The Zen master replied, "We were all women." His answer speaks to the unity of all things and the apparent lack of need to worry about gender discrepancies. *We are all women; we are all men.*

But this begs the question of why we have only the male version of Oneness. Empowered by writing about the forgotten histories of women in Zen, Grace now had a reply to this Zen master, "How many of you women used the ladies room at the Zen conference?"

In *Zen Women*, Grace has "moved beyond the question of why and how female Zen ancestors had been erased from Zen history. I have sought to identify these erased women and put them back in the Zen practice I loved."

Here is one precious example from *Zen Women*. "One morning an old lady experienced kensho (Zen awakening) while cleaning up after breakfast. She rushed over and announced to Hakuin (the famous eighteenth-century Zen master), 'Amida has engulfed my body! The universe radiates! How truly marvelous!' 'Nonsense!' Hakuin retorted. 'Does it shine up your asshole?' The tiny lady gave Hakuin a shove and shouted, 'What do you know about enlightenment?' They both roared with laughter."

BUDDHIST ART

From Temples to Statues

Religions have inspired much of the world's great art, such as Michelangelo's Sistine Chapel and the Taj Mahal. Buddhism has also inspired beautiful and ambitious artwork, from the ephemeral to the enduring. These art forms include painting and sculpture-chocked caves, architecture, *thangkas*, mandalas, statuary, calligraphy, and contemporary art. Buddhist art is some of the most distinctive and recognizable art in the world.

ARCHITECTURE

The beginning of Buddhist architecture can be traced back to King Ashoka in the third century B.C.E. Ashoka built great stupas and pillars in tribute to the Buddha. Two of the most famous pillars are the ones at Sarnath that used to house the Lion Capital (the Buddha was known as "Lion of the Shakyas") and the one in the Lumbini Garden. There are more incredible works of Buddhist architecture than can be listed here, but some of the more outstanding ones deserve special mention.

Stupas

The Buddha died somewhere between 483 and 400 B.C.E. and his remains were quickly taken for custodial protection by King Ajatasattu of Magadha, India. According to legend, the king divided the cremated remains into eight portions and gave each portion to one of eight different kings to protect and cherish. Each king was directed to build a stupa to house the remains, and these stupas were erected all over India and present-day Nepal.

Relics

When the Buddha was cremated, rulers from various kingdoms came quickly to reclaim the relics of his body. Arguments ensued but a Brahmin named Dona was quick to quell the disagreement. His clever speech convinced the kings to divide the relics between them and build stupas to honor the holy Buddha.

King Ashoka was thought to have opened up seven of the eight stupas and relocated the relics of the Buddha to structures that he had subsequently built. The Hill of Sanchi, one of the most well-known Buddhist stupas, is one of Ashoka's most famous creations.

The Hill of Sanchi is a group of Buddhist monuments. The foundation was laid by Ashoka but was later damaged, rebuilt, and added to over the centuries. When two of the stupas on the Hill of Sanchi were excavated in the nineteenth century several of the relic caskets were recovered. Today, relics of the Buddha are scattered and appear in China, Burma, Sri Lanka, India, and elsewhere—fingerbones, teeth, hair, and bone have all been preserved. Three stupas at Sanchi have been recovered.

Another of the greatest works of architecture in Buddhist history is the Borobudur Temple, a stone work of wonder standing in Java, Indonesia. The size of the temple is awe-inspiring, and is made from nearly 200,000 square feet of lava rock. The temple is composed of six rectangular terraces. The top of the structure contains three more circular terraces and a spire stupa forms the top. The temple is thought to have been the Buddhist cultural center in the seventh and eighth centuries.

The Borobudur Temple is a massive structure overlooking the misty mountains and green valleys of Java. The whole structure is in the form of a lotus, a symbol of Buddhism. It also represents the Buddhist cosmos, with realms of desire, form, and formlessness depicted from bottom to top. The lowest level of the structure features 160 carved panels illustrating the joys and horrors of life in the Realm of Desire. There are more than 1,400 scenes in all from top to bottom, with ninety-two Buddha statues for each direction. The structure is a marvel of devotion and endurance. Borobudur has been used for devotional practice for centuries—you can walk around the terraces while meditating, walking clockwise until you reach the top.

The Cave Temples of Ajanta

In western India you can find the cave temples of Ajanta. These "caves" are actually manmade structures carved out of living rock. Hsüan-tsang, the famous Chinese Buddhist pilgrim who traveled in India for sixteen years, first wrote about the Ajanta caves in the eighth century C.E. The caves were originally used as dwellings and meeting houses for Buddhists. Frescoes decorate the cave walls. There are approximately thirty such temple caves, some created as early as 200 B.C.E., and some as late as the seventh century. It is not known who painted the brilliantly depicted scenes from both the Buddha's life and from the Jataka tales, but they are colorful and larger than life. The caves were rediscovered by the British in 1817.

The Magao Caves of Dunhuang

One of the greatest repositories of Buddhist art is found in China amidst the Magao Caves. There are 800 caves, built between the fourth and fourteenth centuries C.E., of which 492 are decorated with murals and statuary. The start of the cave creation is attributed to a Buddhist monk named Yuezun who, in 366 C.E., responded to a vision of a thousand Buddhas by carving a small meditation cell in the rock. Others followed and the practice became more and more ambitious. Emperors would outdo their predecessors with magnificent projects.

It is estimated that the murals cover a half-million feet of wall space. And as for sculptures, there are more than 2,000 of them (reduced from tens of thousands due to plundering).

The Oldest Book

The oldest printed book was found in cave seventeen at Magao. It is a copy of the Diamond Sutra and was printed with woodblock on a sixteen-foot scroll in 868 C.E., nearly 600 years before the Guttenberg Bible. You can visit the scroll at the British Library in London.

These magnificent caves on the Silk Road reflect the great influence that Buddhism had on China, more so than any of the religions that have appeared in China. A recent *National Geographic* article on the caves describes them in this way. "Within the caves, the monochrome and lifelessness of the desert gave way to an exuberance of color and movement. Thousands of Buddhas in every hue radiated across the grotto wall, their robes glinting with imported gold."

The caves employ a staff of 500 and receive a half-million visitors each year. The caves have survived centuries of sandstorms, plundering archeologists, and the Cultural Revolution. It's biggest threat today is the moist breath of its multitude of tourists.

BUDDHIST STATUARY AND IMAGES

The image of the Buddha is familiar worldwide. The first images of the Buddha appeared during the reign of King Kanishka in the first century and were greatly influenced by the Hellenic art coming out of Central Asia. The Buddha image conveys serenity and calm. The proportions of the Buddha are always ideal. Though there is some variation in measurement and scale from school to school and country to country, most Buddha images have the following characteristics:

- The top of the Buddha's head has a raised area that symbolizes enlightened mind.
- The hands and the feet are equal in length and scale.
- The nose is long, straight, and noble.
- There is a mark in the center of the forehead—the Eye of Wisdom.
- The ears are elongated.

Buddha images portray grace and great beauty. One of the most famous Buddha images is Wat Pho (the Temple of the Reclining Buddha), in Thailand. The gold-plated reclining Buddha is more than 150 feet long and 49 feet high and represents the Buddha's paranirvana. The temple grounds contain more than 1,000 Buddha images.

MANDALAS AND SAND PAINTINGS

A sand painting is exactly what it sounds like—a painting made of sand. Sand paintings represent the impermanence of all things. Mandalas are maps of the spiritual world. They are usually represented in artwork as a graphic symbolic pattern. The pattern is usually in the form of a circle with intricate designs within. The patterns are representative of the sacred place where the Buddha or deity abides. They are used for contemplation and meditation and are designed to awaken spiritual potential.

According to Buddhist scholar Michael Willis, *mandala* literally means "circle" or "enclosure," but it represents more than this—it is a sort of cosmic diagram that provides a structure to guide meditation practice. A typical mandala would have outer rings of concentric circles representing the oceans and mountains. Inside these circles would be a square form with four gates, one on each side representing the cardinal directions. Each has its own characteristic color: white for the east, red for the west, green for the north, and yellow for the south. In the middle of the form resides a special meditation deity.

Sand Mandalas

The most spectacular mandalas are also the most ephemeral. Tibetan Buddhists monks will labor for weeks creating an elaborate mandala made of colored sand. These mandalas can be six, eight, or ten feet in diameter. Once completed, the sand is swept away in a closing ritual and then deposited in a nearby body of water.

Willis explains, "Elaborate mandalas painted on cloth scrolls or on temple walls were once common in many parts of the Himalayas, the best preserved examples being found in Bhutan, Nepal, and those parts of India which are culturally Tibetan, such as Ladakh."

Sand paintings are often mandalas. Tibetan lamas create them to promote healing. Sand paintings are made with vegetable-dyed sand, flowers, herbs, grains, stone, and sometimes jewels. A platform is laid out, and once the platform is in place the lama will start a healing ceremony that blesses the area. The sand and other materials are placed on the platform over a period of time in a meditative process. When the sand painting is finished, it is dismantled, demonstrating the impermanence in action. After a ceremony, the sand is swept into a large vessel and deposited in a river or a lake, again with ceremony.

THANGKAS

Thangkas are paintings. They are often done on canvas and turned into scrolls, framed in silk, and hung from a dowel. The dowel can be made of wood with decorative metal knobs on the ends. Thangkas are also often mandalas. They depict images of different deities, such as the bodhisattva Avalokiteshvara or any of the numerous Tibetan deities. As compared to sand painting mandalas, thangkas are a more permanent art form. They are often used as meditative devices and are hung by an altar.

GARDENS

Japanese gardens are some of the most exquisite gardens to be found. Their simplicity, stark beauty, and serenity are moving and inspire peace. For centuries, Japanese Zen masters created gardens out of rocks and sand, raking the sand into patterns that could be destroyed quickly, like the sand paintings, to emphasize the impermanence of all things. These gardens are designed for contemplation and meditation. In a dry element garden, movement can be depicted using sand, and rocks can be used to represent mountains or islands in the sand streams. Bridges are a common element in many Japanese gardens as well.

Garden design under the Japanese became a spiritual activity. Gardens in Zen monasteries became objects for meditation and an appreciation for natural beauty. While constructed, these gardens represent more than human creation. The best-known designer of Zen gardens was Muso Soseki who lived in the thirteenth and fourteenth centuries. Ponds were created to represent the mind, and in one walking garden sharp rocks were juxtaposed with soft moss to represent the confluence of beauty and monastic austerity. Raked rock gardens are also striking examples of Zen symbolism, with rocks representing thoughts in the sea of the mind.

CREATING HAIKUS AND CALLIGRAPHY

Art Forms

Haiku is Japanese poetry form that traditionally follows a pattern of five–seven–five syllables. This is generally a good way for haiku beginners to start but it is not a rigid rule. Instead, it is important that the haiku uses no spare words—no unnecessary words and syllables.

Haikus are written in a moment of inspiration where the self-conscious mind drops and the poet is in touch with the unity of all things. Haiku is a mindfulness meditation. Haikus are about everyday life and usually have a nature theme. One of the lines usually contains a word that indicates the season to which the haiku refers, thereby giving it a sense of time and place. Wild plums, for instance, would indicate summer.

Basho

Basho is known as a great haiku poet. He was born Matsuo Munefusa in seventeenth-century Japan. In his youth, Basho was a samurai but exchanged his sword for his poetry. He lived in a hut made of banana leaves, which is how he came by his pseudonym. *Basho* means "banana leaves."

Haikus do not usually refer to a participant: in other words—no self. This usually extends to mean no adjectives, because adjectives can imply a judge (a beautiful tree implies an opinion, therefore someone who holds the opinion).

Here is an example of haiku from Basho:

Winter rain
falls on the cow-shed;
a cock crows.

Notice that the haiku does not follow the five-seven-five rule but a similar beat is found: three-five-three. Haikus are not intended to be brilliant and pithy. They are strokes of inspiration and honesty coming from the heart. Most of all, haikus are reverent toward the sanctity of the small things, and of everything. Children love to create haiku poetry, which says a lot about the simplicity and honesty to be found in the haiku form.

ZEN ART AND CALLIGRAPHY

Many of the Zen arts trace their origins to China, but they receive their fullest expression in Japan. These art forms include painting, calligraphy, poetry, photography, archery, swordsmanship, tea ceremony, flower arranging, and garden design. Typically, Zen art eschews narrative for an aesthetic sensibility that simultaneously conveys openness and compactness. The aim of the art is to inspire insight rather than devotion. In this way Zen art is similar to a koan.

Zen painting takes as its subjects landscapes, depictions of famous Zen stories, koans, and Zen masters. For example, landscape paintings seek to depict the enormity of the universe and the smallness of humanity in the context of nature.

There is a tradition of art practice within Zen. Art arises spontaneously and manifests the buddha-nature within you. Art practice is mindfulness training. The art relies on a foundation of technical training that is then expressed in spontaneous practice. Zen art tends to be simple, sometimes stark, and always lovely.

Shien

A sequence of ten ox-herding pictures are attributed to Kakuan Shien, twelfth-century Zen master from China. Early ox-herding pictures exist, but Kakuan Shien is known for creating an entire sequence of ten that has survived to this day.

Calligraphy (*Zenga*)

Japanese calligraphy is an art form spiritually expressed through Zen. The artist must be in touch with buddha-nature to create an expression of enlightenment. The brush stroke must come from a union with the world; no separation must exist—no *I* and *pen*, just the act itself.

Japanese calligraphy dates back to the seventh century, where it was part of art practice and meditation in monasteries. Often, the subject of a Japanese calligraphy and painting would be a koan. One of the most common examples of Zenga is the open circle, called *enso*. The simplicity of the enso was particularly popular during the Edo period of Japan in the eighteenth century. Enso symbolized enlightenment, emptiness, and life itself. In the series of ox-herding pictures by Kakuan Shien, for example, the eighth step in the sequence (both ox and self forgotten) is represented by enso.

During the execution of the calligraphy, the slightest hesitation on the part of the artist will cause the ink to blot on the thin rice paper, and the calligraphy will be ruined. Technique is learned and perfected over many years before such spontaneity is possible. Once the boundary between art supplies, art, and self are gone the art can be executed.

FLOWER ARRANGING

Japanese flower arranging is called *ikebana*. Ikebana evolved in Japan over the course of many centuries. The written history of ikebana can be traced back to the fifteenth century, to the first ikebana school. Many years of training are required before someone achieves the technique necessary to perform ikebana well. Many different ways of fastening the flowers into an arrangement are possible, using various techniques. The essence of ikebana is simplicity, and in contrast to Western flower arrangement very few flowers, leaves, and stems are used to achieve the desired effect. Ikebana uses the flowers, the container, and the space around the flower arrangement as part of the artistic impression.

There are different styles of ikebana. Some styles use low containers and the flowers are piled on top. Other styles use tall, narrow vases and the flowers have a tossed-about look to them. Ikebana strives to use seasonal flowers and foliage in a naturalistic presentation. Traditional forms of ikebana use three points to represent the realms of heaven, human, and earth.

BUDDHIST EDUCATION

Training for the Future

Buddhist educational facilities provided educational opportunities across Asia. That tradition continues in the West to this day. Today, Naropa University in Boulder, Colorado, is based on Nalanda University, the ancient Indian university. The mission statement of Naropa University affirms its intention to promote awareness of the moment through intellectual, artistic, and meditative disciplines; to create and foster a learning community that reveals wisdom; to cultivate communication; to stay true to the origins of the original Nalanda University; to encourage integration of modern culture with ancient wisdom; and to remain nonsectarian and "open to all." The Buddhist educational system seems to be as alive today as it was millennia ago.

VISITING MONASTERIES AND RETREAT CENTERS

When laypeople visit monasteries they often wonder how they can be respectful and what behavior is expected of them. Although many people are curious as to what goes on in a Buddhist monastery and would like to speak with the monks or watch a meditation session, they are afraid they will be pestered for donations or be pressured to "convert."

However, you could say that Buddhism is a program of attraction rather than evangelism. Traditionally, Buddhism was a missionary religion, although in the West, Buddhists do not try to convert others to Buddhism. They might speak enthusiastically of their personal practices if asked, but it is highly unlikely that you would be solicited for money or anything else at a monastery or through mail, email, or other means. A donation (dana) might be suggested at certain monasteries, much like a museum will have a suggested donation box in the admission area.

Bring an Offering

If you visit a monastery it is customary to take a small offering, such as a bouquet of flowers or an offering of food. You may also donate money. These are part of the generosity practice (dana) aimed to overcome the fire of greed.

Most monasteries welcome visitors and most visits are free of charge. Classes, retreats, and lectures might charge something to cover meals and lodging, and depending on the institution, instruction may be part of the fee or be addressed separately through dana. Having said this, some retreats have become very expensive and are out of reach to the person of average means. Fancy retreats at spa locations are becoming more and more common. In typical American style, the dharma has become a status symbol in some, but not all, circles. Some monasteries have stores where they sell art, meditation supplies, and clothing to help generate money to support the monastery. Most sitting sessions will be free of charge. Check the Internet for a monastery or Buddhist center near you if you would like to visit. You can probably find information on the website that will put you at ease before you visit. Call ahead or email with any questions you might have. Most centers will have a scholarship program.

BUDDHISM IN THE WEST

A Growing Practice

In the West, Buddha and Buddhism are attractive forces for both personal growth and social change. You can embrace Buddha without embracing Buddhism. Buddha requires no beliefs and no affiliations and so doesn't conflict with your own belief system whether you are devoutly religious or an atheist. Buddha's teachings are universal, transcending time and culture. If you have a mind, then Buddha is relevant to you. Many of the presentations of Buddhism in the West are more Buddha than Buddhism. For example, you will find mindfulness meditation being taught at major medical centers with no Buddhist context or affiliation.

ARE YOU A BUDDHIST?

How do you become a Buddhist? What does it mean to be a card-carrying Buddhist? Buddhism represents a great diversity of traditions, so there is no one way to become a Buddhist and perhaps, ironically, no need to become a "Buddhist." There is a curious situation in America where many teachers who teach Buddhist meditation would not consider themselves "Buddhist" although they lead lives entirely consistent with the principles and practices of this religion. Buddhism in America has become quite popular and many people might identify themselves as such.

One prerequisite to identification as a Buddhist would be to take refuge in the Triple Jewel: the Buddha, the dharma, and the sangha. Buddha is not just the historical person of the Buddha; it is what the

Buddha represents—the potential for awakening that you have. Taking refuge in Buddha is not idolatry. Buddhists look to the Buddha as a role model, especially in America (although in Asian contexts it can appear that people are really praying to the Buddha as a god by requesting intercessory prayers). Dharma is the body of teachings that the Buddha taught and the truths that these teachings point to. Sometimes dharma is translated as "The Way"—the way to live to get beyond suffering. Sangha is the community of like-minded practitioners on the same path—it is the people you might practice with at a local meditation gathering in your community, such as a Zen Temple, and all the people all over the world stretching back in time 2,500 years. Taking refuge is an initiation into an awakened life. It is like getting on a raft that will carry you across the river of samsara (endless suffering).

You can also join a sangha by becoming a monk. Monastic initiation is more involved than lay initiation. Some Americans choose to become a monk or a nun in one of these Asian traditions. To do this, you would have to renounce aspects of your life and take on the monastic vows. In the Zen tradition, you would shave your head and devote yourself to a life of service to your Zen master and your zendo (Zen Temple). There is also lay ordination. Initiation into the Triple Jewel is, perhaps, the closest these diverse traditions have to a universal initiation. For most religions, becoming a member of that religion requires adopting a set of beliefs and a corresponding faith in those beliefs. Buddhism is different in this way. There are some core principles that reflect the teachings of the Buddha and you must be on board with these to be considered a "Buddhist," but these are not articles of faith, like believing in a virgin birth, a creator god, or even an enlightened prophet. They are more practical. Noted Buddhist author and scholar Stephen Batchelor suggests there can be Buddhism without beliefs in ideas such as rebirth.

WHAT MAKES YOU *NOT* A BUDDHIST

Dzongsar Jamyang Khyentse Rinpoche, author of *What Makes You Not a Buddhist*, provides four criteria to consider. To be a Buddhist, one must believe in all four of the following tenets or seals: all compounded things are impermanent; all emotions are pain; all things have no inherent existence; and nirvana is beyond all concepts. While these might be considered "beliefs," each is based on direct experience, the kind of experience that can arise from your practice of meditation. If you meditate, you will notice that things are constantly changing—the quality of your breathing, the energy in your body, and the ceaseless flow of thoughts in your mind. The tenet that "all emotions are pain" seems harder to accept. After all, joy is not "painful." But this joy won't last (since everything is impermanent), and somewhere in the back of your mind there is the recognition and fear that this experience won't last. Emotions, in this case, might be distinguished from feelings, with emotions being a complex of intense feelings that are suffused with thoughts and embedded in a story that eventually has something to do with desire. "All things have no inherent existence" is the teaching on emptiness, and again is less a belief than an experience that arises in meditation. "Nirvana is beyond all concepts" can also be experienced in meditation.

If you like being a Buddhist because of the colorful rituals and the exotic association with Asian cultures, and the message of compassion and peace, but don't "get" these four seals, Rinpoche suggests you are not a Buddhist in the important sense of being a Buddhist. In other words, to be a Buddhist is to understand Buddhist psychology—to have a direct experience of what the Buddha discovered and that you can discover if you devote yourself to any of the Buddhist meditation practices.

SECULAR BUDDHISM

A Western Dharma

Stephen Batchelor is the leading voice of a growing movement toward secular Buddhism. His books, spanning the last twenty years from *Buddhism Without Beliefs* to his recent *Secular Buddhism,* articulate a vision of the Buddha's teachings that are free from dogma, ritual, and metaphysical beliefs. Separating Buddha from the Buddhist traditions that emerged from his teachings retains a rich set of practices—centered on the Four Noble Truths. Batchelor recommends these as a series of tasks to complete rather than a set of beliefs. The goal of these four tasks is not to achieve some ultimate spiritual experience but, rather, to flourish in one's life in the here and now.

INNOVATIVE CONTRIBUTIONS

Little can be known about the Buddha's teachings with absolute certainty. They were persevered orally for centuries until they were written down by the Buddhist councils. None of these original writings still exist and scholars must rely upon commentaries and translations written centuries later. One approach to understanding the Buddha is to try to understand the worldview that he was teaching within. At the time in ancient India, beliefs in karma, rebirth, and concerns over the ultimate reality of self and reality were prevalent. The Buddha would have had to use this language to reach his audiences (through skillful means). Whether he believed these things or not, he didn't find them useful for thriving in one's life. It is more useful to look at what the Buddha's unique contributions were. Batchelor identifies these four:

1. Conditionality—the observation that what happens now gives rise to what happens later, whether these are events in the world or mental events. Things don't occur randomly; it's cause and effect.
2. The practice of the Four Noble Truths (or tasks).
3. The central importance of mindfulness and mindfulness meditation.
4. An emphasis on self-reliance over the authority of priests, dogma, or speculative beliefs.

"A great deal of modern education and psychotherapy consists of making people aware that they are responsible for themselves. In fact, we consider that it constitutes a large part of what we mean by becoming a mature person. It is amazing that someone should have promulgated this idea in the fifth century B.C.E., and hardly less remarkable that he found followers."

—Noted Buddhist scholar Richard Gombrich

These four unique contributions comprise a Buddhism that is secular, psychological, and personal. It also lends itself to a contemporary scientific worldview.

A SCIENTIFIC WESTERN BUDDHISM

Mindfulness meditation has been brought into the laboratory and has been the subject of hundreds of research studies, many focusing on neuroimaging. There is an explosion of interest in what is happening in the brain both functionally in terms of attention and structurally in terms of how the brain changes in response to meditation. These studies are still in their infancy but they hold great promise toward understanding the positive effects of meditation.

Traditional Buddhists have been critical of this scientific study of Buddhism arguing that it will corrupt, distort, or dilute Buddhism since it is removed from its ethical context. Nevertheless, the research agenda continues and might be the emergence of a contemporary dharma (version of Buddhism) that is unique to the secular scientific Western world.

As Buddhism spread throughout Asia, it always changed in dramatic ways as it integrated with the host culture. As Buddhism comes to the West, it will also change by integrating the values of this culture. These include secularism, science, and materialism. Despite the protests of traditionalists, the Buddha might approve the scientific study of his teachings because it is consistent with the practical approach that he advocated.

To the extent that scholars such as Stephen Batchelor, John Peacock, and Richard Gombrich can unearth the intentions of the Buddha (separate from Buddhist religions that followed), he appears pragmatic with an attitude consistent with the stance of science—test things out for yourself rather than accepting anything on authority, tradition, or faith.

The shape of Western dharma will, no doubt, evolve in the future to arrive at its unique historical form. In the meantime, there is a rich and growing secular tradition available to those who do not wish to engage in any of the formal Buddhisms that are available. To be secular, you would still seek to understand the influence of the three fires and to work to undermine their influence. You would seek nirvana not as some mystical abstraction but as an experience in the here and now that is mindful, compassionate, and filled with equanimity.

MINDFULNESS IN ALL THINGS

Emotional Intelligence

Mindfulness can be thought of as a skillful way of engaging with your emotional life, which is critical to functioning in the world. According to researchers John D. Mayer, Peter Salovey, and David R. Caruso, "emotional intelligence" (EI) is composed of four features:

1. Perceiving emotions accurately in oneself and others
2. Using emotions to facilitate thinking
3. Understanding emotions, emotional language, and the signals conveyed by emotions
4. Managing emotions so as to attain specific goals

Emotional intelligence is the "ability to engage in sophisticated information processing about one's own and others' emotions and the ability to use this information as a guide to thinking and behavior. That is, individuals high in EI pay attention to, use, understand, and manage emotions, and these skills serve adaptive functions that potentially benefit themselves and others." Emotional intelligence was popularized by Daniel Goleman's book by that name. As you will see, EI can be directly affected by meditation in areas such as empathy and emotional regulation.

NINE BENEFITS OF MINDFULNESS MEDITATION

Mindfulness can bring your brain into an integrated state of harmony, balancing chaos on the one hand and rigidity on the other.

This scientific wisdom is brought to you by neuroscientist, Daniel Siegel, author of several important books, including *The Developing Mind, The Mindful Brain, Mindsight*, and *The Mindful Therapist*. The middle prefrontal cortex (a portion of the newest part of the brain evolution-wise, located behind the forehead and known as the "rational brain"—in contrast to the "emotional brain" that is older evolutionarily) is critical to the following nine functions:

- Bodily regulation
- Attunement
- Emotional balance
- Response flexibility
- Downregulation of fear
- Insight
- Empathy
- Morality
- Intuition

Research suggests that each of these functions is positively affected by meditation. When you meditate, your prefrontal cortex will change. It will become thicker in places, indicating new neural connections and perhaps even new neurons. It will be more efficient and more integrated.

Bodily Regulation

Bodily regulation is accomplished by regulating arousal and relaxation through the sympathetic and parasympathetic branches of the autonomic nervous system (think of the gas pedal and a brake in a car). If you are overly stressed or anxious, your sympathetic nervous system is overly active—think of a lead foot on the gas pedal;

the car lurches forward and uses a lot of gas. Mindfulness helps to regulate the sympathetic nervous system, making it less reactive (no more lead foot) so that you can drive the car more slowly. This cuts down on the wear and tear of your body and reduces the risk for long-term health problems.

Attunement

Attunement is being connected to others, or being "in tune." By being mindful you can better connect to others because you are more present and less preoccupied with your own story. Attunement sows the seeds of compassion. Attunement provides the optimal environment for babies to develop in; healthy development happens when caregivers are attuned with their babies.

Emotional Balance

Emotional balance refers to how you engage with experiences. It balances apathy on the one hand and feeling overwhelmed on the other. Like bodily regulation, it's a Goldilocks phenomenon: not too much and not too little. This is the optimal place for neural integration. Like bodily regulation, mindfulness helps you to be more nuanced and less clumsy in your emotional responses. This will come in handy in your relationships and when dealing with the day-to-day frustrations of life.

Response Flexibility

Response flexibility refers to the pause that can develop between a stimulus and response. It aims at the impulsive reactions that often occur in response to a stimulus. This pause comes from mindful awareness and can help you to be less impulsive and less destructive with what you say and do.

Downregulation of Fear

The emotional brain, which is responsible for emotions like fear and anger, has the job of keeping you safe. It does so by figuring out what you should be paying attention to. It is prone to make mistakes that err on the side of caution. "Is that a snake or a stick? Let's assume it's a snake and let's get the hell out of here." That kind of mistake is less costly than guessing wrong. It takes longer to recover from a snakebite than to catch your breath for running away for no good reason.

To be more accurate in detecting what should really get your precious attention resources, the prefrontal cortex (the rational brain) needs to have more nerve fibers going from the rational brain to the emotional brain to tell it, "Hey, it's a false alarm." This is accomplished through the development of inhibitory nerve fibers that go from the middle prefrontal cortex to structures like the amygdala in the emotional brain (limbic system). The practice of mindfulness helps you develop those pathways.

Insight

Insight refers to what Siegel calls mental time travel, or what you might call imagination. Mindfulness can help you to refine this capacity in the service of living skillfully rather than being subjected to out-of-control worry, regret, and self-criticism. If you are not using your imagination for these destructive purposes, it will be free to be creative.

Empathy

Empathy, or what Siegel calls "mindsight," refers to the ability to take the perspective of the other. Obviously, this is connected to compassion and once again hinges upon the ability to transcend your own self-preoccupied stories to meet the person you are with where they are. While some people are naturally more empathic than others, you are not stuck in the place where you are. As with all of these functions, empathy is a trainable skill. The more you meditate the more empathic you can become.

Morality

Morality is also a function of the middle prefrontal cortex and includes not just your ability to be moral in public settings but also in private. As you already know, morality or ethics is a cornerstone of Buddhist teaching and practice, so it may not be a surprise to find morality showing up on this list too. Buddhist meditation practice helps you to discern skillful from unskillful actions in all domains. In the context of morality, this may require inhibiting an impulse, or inserting a pause before you say something.

Intuition

Intuition is the capacity to access the wisdom of the body by monitoring your bodily sensations. For example, a brain structure called the insula has a map of the interior body, and studies have found the insula gets thicker with meditation practice. The more you meditate the more aware you will be of your body. This awareness can help you to cope with whatever the body is experiencing, whether that is pain, anxiety, or discomfort.

Before he took an interest in mindfulness, Siegel independently came up with the same list of brain functions as mindfulness researchers had compiled. And it's not just brain researchers; this list has been utilized in many spiritual traditions since ancient times. When you recognize the plasticity of the brain (that is, its capacity to change in response to experience) you can understand why you respond to certain situations the way that you do. Your previous conditioning will cause you to react in sometimes-harmful ways. However, it is your responsibility (and potential) to change these conditionings through mindfulness and meditation. The middle prefrontal cortex develops optimally in an interpersonally attuned environment during infancy. Mindfulness provides the possibility of self-attunement to affect these same brain areas. So sit down and change your brain! (For more information visit: http://drdansiegel.com.)

MINDFUL YOGA
Easing Pain and Suffering

Siddhartha Gotama was an accomplished yogi before he became the Buddha. The word "yoga" derives from the verb *yuj*: "to yoke" or "to bind together." The yogi seeks to yoke body and mind and the future and past with the present moment. Yoga has become enormously popular in the United States with an emphasis on the physical postures or *asanas*. Yet, according to Frank Jude Boccio in his book, *Mindfulness Yoga,* only three of Patanjali's 195 aphorisms deal with asana.

Patanjali

Patanjali is the author of the *Yoga Sutras*, an important text for many of the yogas practiced today, especially Ashtanga Yoga. He lived in the second century B.C.E. These sutras outline an eight-limbed system for yoga. One of the principle purposes of performing yoga asanas (postures) is to prepare the body for meditation.

Like any activity, yoga can be done with or without mindfulness. However, when done with mindfulness, yoga can be a powerful practice for alleviating chronic pain and suffering. Yoga is an integral component in Mindfulness-Based Stress Reduction (MBSR), where the emphasis is not on performing the postures correctly or getting a great workout. The emphasis, rather, is on bringing mindfulness to the postures where they are done very slowly. Mindful yoga provides you with an opportunity to take mindfulness into motion and facilitates its integration into daily life.

BUDDHISTS AS ACTIVISTS

Healing the World

Melvin McLeod is the editor of the book *Mindful Politics*. "Politics is really about how we live together as human beings, and all spiritual practices point to one simple but profound truth about human life— that only love leads to peace, hatred never does. This is as true for nations as it is for individuals."

His proposed political platform (if the Buddha was a politician he might base his politics on the Four Immeasurables) states:

May all sentient beings enjoy happiness and the root of happiness.
May they be free from suffering and the root of suffering.
May they not be separated from the great happiness devoid of suffering.
May they dwell in the great equanimity free of passion, aggression, and ignorance.

Politics is emotions gone awry—vengeance, war, persecution of difference. The dualistic and false sense of "us" versus "them" underlies much of the conflict. As Buddhism, particularly through mindfulness, promotes emotional and social intelligences, it might have something to offer the world an an antidote to hostility, inequity, and damage. The dualistic and false sense of "us" versus "them" underlies much of the conflict. If everyone is not in this all together then there is the risk of being divided one against another. According to McLeod the keys to change are forgiveness, awareness, kindness, and selflessness. Politics is ultimately about relationships and all relationships brook in power and conflict. How will these conflicts be resolved? With mindful awareness or through the perpetuation of the three fires.

Individual transformation is the prerequisite for societal transformation. The first step is not to save the world, but to save yourself. If everyone works to limit or even eliminate hatred, greed, and ignorance, then the world will be made a better place through the aggregation of this absence.

"When we talk about preservation of the environment, it is related to many other things. Ultimately, the decision must come from the human heart. The key point is to have a genuine sense of universal responsibility, based on love and compassion, and clear awareness."

—The Dalai Lama

Consider this statement from Buddhist monk and Vietnam veteran Claude Anshin Thomas in his book *At Hell's Gate: A Soldier's Journey from War to Peace*: "Peace is not an idea. Peace is not a political movement, not a theory or a dogma. Peace is a way of life: living mindfully in the present moment . . . It is not a question of politics, but of actions. It is not a matter of improving a political system or even taking care of homeless people alone. These are valuable but will not alone end war and suffering. We must simply stop the endless wars that rage within . . . Imagine, if everyone stopped the war in themselves—there would be no seeds from which war could grow."

ENGAGED BUDDHISM IN ACTION

Here are two examples of American Zen teachers who took their practice out of the zendo to serve their communities and the sangha.

Bernard Tetsugen Glassman

Bernard Tetsugen Glassman is one of America's most provocative Zen teachers and promoters of Engaged Buddhism. In 1982 he founded the Greyston Bakery in New York City. His idea was to start a business that would employ the members of his sangha—allowing them to leave their day jobs—so they could concentrate more fully on their practice and contribute to the practice of Engaged Buddhism. In 1993 the Greyston Foundation, a nonprofit corporation, was created to oversee social improvement programs. Profits from the bakery filter through the foundation, supporting its social development work for the poor and afflicted. Greyston helps the homeless, the jobless, and provides childcare, healthcare, and living assistance for people with HIV/AIDS.

"So for me the question became, 'What are the forms in business, social action, and peacemaking that can help us see the oneness in society, the interdependence in life?'"

—Roshi Bernie Glassman

When Greyston was established, Roshi Glassman (with Roshi Sandra Holmes) then went on to create an order of Zen practitioners devoted to the cause of peace. The Zen Peacemaker Order subsequently emerged. The Peacemaker Community is now an international peacemaking group with members of the world's five major religions. The network includes organizations such as Greyston Mandala, Prison Dharma Network, and Upaya Zen Center in the United States; StadtRaum in Germany; Mexico City Village in Mexico; La Rete d'Indra in Italy; and Shanti Relief Committee in Japan.

Joan Jiko Halifax

Roshi Joan Jiko Halifax is a student of Thich Nhat Hanh, a founding member of the Zen Peacemaker Order, and founder and roshi of the Upaya Zen Center in Santa Fe, New Mexico. She is an author and activist and is greatly respected for her work with the dying. Upaya programs include the Project on Being with Dying, the Partners Program, the Prison Outreach Project, and the Kailash Education Fund.

Working with the Dying

Frank Ostaseki is the founder of the Metta Institute and the Zen Hospice project. He says of working with the dying, "The eyes of a dying patient are the clearest mirrors I have ever looked into. They show me myself in a way that nothing else can. They show me my deepest clinging, my aversion, and something else—an undying love."

The Project on Being with Dying is a program aimed at helping caregivers work with dying people, to change their relationship to both the dying and living. A focus of the program is the training of healthcare professionals. These professionals take their work with the dying back to their own institutions where they can teach these practices to other healthcare professionals. The Partners Program matches dying people with caregivers they need, complementing the help of hospice workers and medical professionals. The Prison Outreach Project offers mindfulness training to inmates in the Mexico prison system, aiming to reduce stress in prison. The Kailash Education Fund is aimed at providing educational opportunities to some of the poorest children in Nepal.

BUDDHA IN JAIL

The United States imprisons more of its citizens than any other country in the world. Buddhism has ventured into the prison system in the United States. Shugen Sensei is the director of the National Buddhist Prison Sangha (NBPS) that started in 1984 with John Daido Loori. Their aim is to teach inmates meditation.

Prison can also provide the opportunity for awakening as portrayed in the compelling memoir, *Razor-Wire Dharma* by Calvin Malone. In it, he describes the mundane experience of eating an apple, an apple that stood out from the usual horrible prison food. "Breathing in I smelled *apple*, breathing out *the universe*. Everything there is or ever was was contained in this apple . . . I could see it with the wild exactness of shattered glass. The answer and the question were there in the apple. I was feeling an inexplicable joy, while at the same time, keenly aware. I never before felt better in my life. I realized this moment was as good as it gets."

The Buddha's teachings offer this form of radical freedom: that the happiest moment of your life could occur during a prison sentence, that true happiness could arise from the simple beauty of an apple, a living thing connected to everything else in the entire universe.

The pioneering work that brought Buddha into prison was conducted by S.N. Goenka at the Tihar Jail in New Delhi, India. This prison was considered the most dangerous prison on earth before his work there; torture and murder were commonplace. A visionary warden, Kiran Bedi, embraced Goenka's aspirations to teach the inmates vipassana meditation. The Vipassana Prison Trust (VPT) teaches vipassana courses to Tihar inmates, a thousand at a time, and teaches in prisons in Israel, New Zealand, Mongolia, Taiwan, Thailand, the United Kingdom, and the United States.

MINDFULNESS IN HEALTHCARE

One of the most significant Buddhist influences in the West does not call itself Buddhist at all. This takes the form of mindfulness in healthcare. Every day around the United States and the rest of the Western world medical patients with chronic pain and other debilitating conditions engage in the same meditation that the Buddha did centuries ago.

The center for this worldwide movement resides in Worcester, Massachusetts, at the Center for Mindfulness in Medicine, Healthcare, and Society, founded by Jon Kabat-Zinn in 1979. Since that time, hundreds of thousands of people have been introduced to Buddha outside the context of formal Buddhism. Almost every major medical center in the United States has a program for Mindfulness-Based Stress Reduction (MBSR) and hundreds of professionals worldwide who do this work. These include programs and professionals at prestigious university hospitals such as Harvard and Duke Medical Schools. This is, perhaps, the premiere and most widespread application of Buddhism, albeit in secular form, in the world.

This practice helps people from all walks of life and from all religious traditions. Since MBSR patients are not being trained in Buddhism, they carry on with whatever beliefs and practices they have. What makes MBSR so special is that it has translated the Buddha's teaching into an effective, practical, and readily learned, eight-week format. More than thirty years of research has confirmed its effectiveness in reducing stress, improving coping, and helping patients to get on with their lives.

BUDDHISM IN DAILY LIFE

Living an Awakened Life

Meditation and all the Buddha's wisdom would not be of much value if it stayed on the cushion. Meditation trains you for living an awakened life.

MINDFULNESS

In *The Greater Discourse on the Foundations of Mindfulness*, the Buddha set forth the practice of mindfulness for his students:

> There is, Monks, this one way to the purification of beings, for the overcoming of sorrow and distress, for the disappearance of pain and sadness, for the gaining of the right path, for the realization of Nirvana—that is to say the four foundations of mindfulness.
> What are the four? Here, monks, a monk abides contemplating body as a body, ardent, clearly aware and mindful, having put aside hankering and fretting for the world; he abides contemplating feelings as feelings … he abides contemplating mind as mind … he abides contemplating mind-objects as mind-objects, ardent, clearly aware and mindful, having put aside hankering and fretting for the world.

Meditation practice helps you to be mindful in daily life so that you can be awake to what you experience and do. It is easy to get caught up in stories about the future and the past, and sometimes these stories turn to worry and regret. You may find yourself commenting, and more likely complaining, about the present but not actually paying attention to it. To be awake is to be mindful; paying attention to the reality of this moment as it is happening without judgment or storytelling. To be mindful is to break the habit of automatic pilot and following every impulse that arises. To be mindful is to be awake in movement: in eating, eliminating, driving, working, loving, and whatever else you do during your day.

To be mindful you try to give full attention to your lived experience. As William James said more than one hundred years ago, "The intellectual life of man consists almost wholly of his substitution of a conceptual order for the perceptual order in which his experience originally lives." To be mindful is to reorient the perceptual away from the conceptual, storytelling aspects of the mind. To be mindful you must pay attention to what you see, hear, taste, smell, and most important, the sensations you feel in your body. You must be aware how your mind generates thoughts in the form of stories, images and memories, and emotions (and all the possible combinations of these). The fruit of meditation practice on the cushion and all the techniques described so far is to facilitate this mindful awareness in daily life.

"When we see a red light . . . we can thank it, because it is a bodhisattva helping us return to the present moment . . . We may have thought of it as an enemy, preventing us from achieving our goal. But now we know the red light is our friend . . . calling us to return to the present moment where we can meet with life, joy, and peace."

—Thich Nhat Hanh

You should take your practice with you into everything you do. Vietnamese Zen master Thich Nhat Hanh provides mindfulness exercises in his wonderful book, *The Miracle of Mindfulness*. Here are a few of his suggestions that you can use during the day:

- Measure your breath by your footsteps.
- Count your breaths.
- Set aside a day of mindfulness.
- Half-smile.
- Follow your breath while having a conversation.

Strive to become mindful in every part of your life. When you are eating, eat. When you are walking, walk. When you are making love, make love. When you are cooking, cook. Be there in the moment, each and every moment. The moment is all you have. *This* moment.

The art of meditation is a way to wake up to the world. You can learn new ways to see your troubles and your pain, and bring true wisdom to our life. As American vipassana teacher Jack Kornfield relates in *A Path with Heart*, attention is like training a puppy. You sit the puppy down and tell him to stay, but the puppy immediately gets up and runs away. So you sit the puppy back down again and tell him to stay. And the puppy runs away. Sometimes he runs away and poops in the corner.

It is the same with your mind. You tell your mind to sit still and it is off to the corner to make a mess, and so you must start over and over again. With mindfulness, you can come back to the present moment in a matter-of-fact way, just picking up where you left off. You wouldn't yell at the puppy, so try not to yell at yourself. All minds wander.

Anything worthwhile requires effort, and meditation practice is a worthwhile endeavor. Sometimes practice will flow fluently and at other times it will be a struggle. It is at those times when a community and a teacher are helpful, because they can provide you with support and keep you on track. Once you have been practicing for a while you will start to taste the fruits of your labor and have glimpses of something beyond the stories about yourself. You might even taste that sense of no self the Buddha talked about as you experience yourself as a moment-to-moment process rather than as a "thing" that needs to be protected and constantly convinced of its worth. Enjoy your practice and keep at it!

CONTEMPLATIVE EDUCATION

Mindfulness is not just beneficial for adults. Why not start with children when they are young? Why not bring mindfulness into the schools? The increasing popularity of mindfulness from healthcare is filtering into the education system. Linda Lantieri, founder of The Inner Resilience Program in New York City, finds that "students who engage in mindfulness practice seem to experience reduced stress and acting-out behaviors and increased coping skills, as well as enhanced concentration and an increased sense that the classroom is a community." Other voices in contemplative education include David Forbes, author of *Boyz 2 Buddhas*, and Deborah Schoeberlein, author of *Mindful Teaching and Teaching Mindfulness: A Guide for Anyone Who Teaches Anything.*

GARDENING

Gardening itself can be an act of meditation. This is portrayed in the book *The Meditative Gardener* by Cheryl Wilfong. Dropping your preoccupation with the future and the past seems more possible with hands immersed in earth and your smile exposed to the sun.

When you garden you connect with your environment in a powerful way. You become intimate with the cycle of life. You can notice the change in the seasons and how each season blends into the next. Spring starts in winter with buds showing through the snow, and leaves start to fall in late summer. The insects have their own life cycles and agendas, and in watching the earthworms and the ants, you can see a larger pattern to life. You can see the interconnection of the roots and the soil, and the creatures and rain. You can eat that which you have grown yourself and feel connected to the earth in a way you may have never known before. Gardening is a meditative act and an affirmation of life.

Try sitting in a garden and practicing breathing meditation. Moments of wakefulness may come as you drop your stories and notice the life around you. Lose yourself in the sound of the birds, the delicate tapping of the rain on leaves. Hear the movement of water and the flow of a gentle breeze. Anyone who spends time outdoors knows the connection between every living thing on earth.

MINDFULNESS IN SPORT AND EXERCISE

All athletes have experienced a meditative state worthy of a Buddha. Sometimes athletic activities pull you into a natural state of mindfulness. Sport becomes a form of meditation when you engage it with your full attention. Understanding mindfulness and mindfulness meditation can help to bring you closer to the experience of sport.

This phenomenon can be called sport-samadhi (recall that samadhi is the Sanskrit term for meditative concentration). This type of focused and absorbed concentration is likely familiar to anyone who has slid down a snow-covered mountain at high speed, pushed the pain barrier on a long-distance run, felt at one with their kayak as it shot a set of rapids, or ripped a phat wave on a surfboard. The talking mind becomes quiet and is fully absorbed in the action of the moment. You are not lost in thoughts about the past and worries or planning for the future. You are not telling stories about the activity or anything else. You are present. There is a steady living presence in the fullness of the moment. This is the state of mindfulness. Mindfulness can be thrilling even if the activity is rather ordinary.

Surfing for Enlightenment

Get on a surfboard to attain enlightenment! Jaimal Yogis suggests surfing as a spiritual path in his poignant and deep memoir, *Saltwater Buddha: A Surfer's Quest to Find Zen on the Sea*. He quotes Suzuki Roshi, "Waves are the practice of water. To speak of waves apart from water and water apart from waves is a delusion."

Nongravity sports such as road running, road biking, and swimming offer a ready opportunity to full body awareness. Instead of a gravity-induced absorption, the immersion in the present moment includes the entire body. Take running, for instance, where you can experience a moment-to-moment connection with your total body experience, even when this experience includes pain and discomfort. The challenge is to stay with the experience at the level of sensation. That is, experiencing it as a pattern of gross and pointed sensations instead of labeling it as "pain." However, the mind has a tendency to move you out of the moment of experiencing sensation and perception and into evaluating and judging the experience. Ultimately, you start to tell stories about the experience: "I can't take this anymore." When you can be mindful of the present, the artificial distinctions between mind and body disappear and yield to an awareness of being.

Mindfulness and sport-samadhi can also impact how you deal with exertion and the limits of your body. If you are running uphill and are engaged in a future-oriented conversation, you will be more apt to give up and not push through the pain and discomfort of that exertion. This future-oriented story may be mindless chatter, or it can also be focused on the activity itself. For instance, you might look up the hill and think, "My god, that's a long way up; I'll never be able to stomach that." This self-talk is very different than staying with the experience of embodiment at that moment. The truth is that running, when it becomes an experience lived in the moment, is a succession of moments; and as intense as those moments may be when attention is focused on now instead of moments from now, the crush of the future is relieved.

You will get a lot more out of yourself by staying in the moment and feeling the sensations rather than thinking about them. This is not the same as gutting through the experience of what might be called pain. While exercising, you should listen to your body so as to extract any vital information out of the sensations and perceptions you are having. Pay attention so that you can know the difference between sensations that can be pushed through and those that should be respected.

Sport, like life, can be joyful. And some of this joy comes from the quality of attention you bring to the sport, in addition to the activity being fun.

SPIRITUAL MATERIALISM

Avoiding the Trap

Being in such a consumer culture you may be at risk for consumerizing your spirituality. Is Buddhism immune from such consumption? Buddhist nun, author, and teacher Thubten Chodron warns that "when we turn to spirituality, we may think that we're leaving behind the corruption of the world for higher purposes. But our old ways of thinking do not disappear; they follow us, coloring the way we approach spiritual practice."

Chögyam Trungpa Rinpoche says in his classic work *Cutting Through Spiritual Materialism*, "We have come here to learn about spirituality. I trust the genuine quality of this search but we must question its nature. The problem is that ego can convert anything to its own use, even spirituality. Ego is constantly attempting to acquire and apply the teachings of spirituality for its own benefit. We become skillful actors, and while playing deaf and dumb to the real meaning of the teachings, we find some comfort in pretending to follow the path. This rationalization of the spiritual path and one's actions must be cut through if true spirituality is to be realized."

Buddhism is not exempt from such concerns. Just look at any issue of *Lion's Roar* (previously *Shambhala Sun*), a bimonthly magazine devoted to the Buddhist viewpoint. It is filled with beautiful and enticing ads for teachings and dharma paraphernalia—meditation cushions, bells, statues, you name it. If not careful, you can become attached to nonattachment. You can become identified with nonidentification. You can get lost in spiritual materialism. A cartoon depicts a mother and her child exiting a burning house via an emergency ladder. The mother urges, "Simon, don't forget

Mommy's yoga mat." Buddhist monks have been spotted wearing Gucci slippers and gold Rolexes. No one is immune from the allure of having things; the problem arises when your sense of okay-ness is dependent on having these things. Everyone must proceed with eternal vigilance in order to be free.

The sheer abundance of teachings that are now available in the West may be both a blessing and curse. The blessing is the accessibility of the dharma in unprecedented ways, including the Internet. The curse is that such abundance may encourage consumerist attitudes. You may find yourself dining at the spiritual smorgasbord, taking a little of this and a little of that and creating a pastiche of teachings that serve your ego's needs and not the needs of true awakening. Instant gratification can be a trap. In today's world, you don't have to work hard to get access to the teachings. You don't need to walk across a high Himalayan mountain pass; you don't need to sit waiting outside the gates of the Zen temple for days. You are a consumer with spiritual "dollars" to spend. In urban centers the choices can be dizzying and the customer is always right. One danger is that if you don't like what you see in yourself by working with one teacher, you can just go down the street to another teacher. Another danger is idealization. The honeymoon period can be ecstatic, expansive, and promising. But just like a good marriage, to get any spiritual attainment you need to stick around once disillusionment sets in. All teachers, including the Buddha, are human.

Convenience is another consideration for spiritual materialism. Consumer culture is designed to make life more convenient or more of something (faster, cooler, healthier, and so forth). When you are in distress you may recognize the increased need for practice, but can you sustain this commitment without a crisis? Meditation is hard. It takes time and if you practice for prolonged periods, it can be physically uncomfortable and, mentally, may bring up things you'd rather not face. There is no quick fix and you need to be careful about seeking shortcuts.

If you do put in the effort, a final aspect of spiritual materialism to consider is what might be called "spiritual Olympics" or "the one with the most spiritual toys wins." You can identify with how prodigious your sitting practice is, how many retreats you've been on, and how many vows you've taken and teachings you've received. Is this any different than showing off your BMW to your neighbor? Is this any different than keeping up with the Joneses? Henry David Thoreau warned us not to identify with the "clothes" of any new activity but to try to be different in how we engage with activity. He said, "beware of any activity that requires new clothes, rather than a new wearer of clothes."

DIVING IN

The Silent Meditation Retreat

The traditional way to learn Theravada-style meditation is by way of a ten-day silent meditation retreat. If you go to one of these retreats, you will experience both shamatha and vipassana. The first three days are devoted to shamatha, focusing on the breath. Depending on the teacher's tradition, this focus may be very narrow (for example, just on the tip of your nose), or the focus may be broader and examine any aspect of the breathing process.

Regardless, the instructions will be clear and straightforward: whenever you find your attention moving away from the sensations of your breathing, bring your attention back. This is what you should expect to happen whenever you meditate. You will place your focus on your breathing, but within a few moments your focus will be somewhere else—into the future or past, or engaged in a commentary about the present. Your mind might become engaged with talking thoughts, or get lost in images, or be awash in emotions, or might entertain sights and sounds, or could fixate on other bodily sensations. This is quite normal.

It can be a source of frustration if you think your mind should be perfectly behaved and never wander. So don't be frustrated. It will wander. The method for controlling this wandering is to keep repeating the process: notice that your attention has moved away from the breath and then bring it back (without adding any criticism of your mental focusing powers).

In the retreat environment, this exclusive focus on breathing will be maintained for three days. You arise early in the morning and engage in multiple meditation periods throughout the day.

Depending on the tradition and the instructor, walking meditation may be interspersed with sitting meditation. Breaks are taken for meals, and these meals are a continuation of practice, the practice of mindful eating.

You may also have the opportunity to do work practice where you do a yogi job such as sweeping floors or washing dishes. The invitation is to be mindful as you do these activities. A typical retreat day may involve over ten hours of formal meditation practice with the remainder of the day engaged with informal practice.

In the Burmese tradition as was taught by the late S.N. Goenka, only sitting meditation is practiced. On breaks, you can walk, but this is not slow walking meditation practice. Goenka asked participants to give up all other practices for the ten days of the retreat so that they can intensify their experience of mindfulness. He will encourage you (still even after his death through videotaped dharma talks) to "work diligently, ardently, patiently and persistently, and you will be bound to be successful."

After establishing a firm foundation of concentration (shamatha) through three days of breathing practice, the remainder of the retreat will be devoted to exploring sensations arising in the body (Burmese tradition) or any arising of phenomena, especially bodily sensations (Thai tradition).

The ten-day retreat is an arduous undertaking. It might be one of the most difficult experiences of your life and the most valuable. It's hard to sit for all those hours without physical discomfort and even pain. However, the retreat becomes a crucible for self-knowledge. Each time you practice mindfulness meditation, you cultivate an intimacy with your own experience and doing so intensively on retreat will give you a very rare opportunity to get to know yourself that is difficult to achieve in everyday life with all its distractions. For this reason, the retreat environment employs what is called "Noble Silence." This means no unnecessary talking (for example, you can talk to a staff member if needed; some retreats have question-and-answer periods and interviews with teachers).

The goal is to disengage from typical discourse, and this includes engaging in eye contact and other nonverbal interactions with others. The retreat environment is an opportunity to, as the Buddha said, "become an island unto yourself." Also suspended for the duration of the retreat are writing, reading, and of course there are no televisions or telephones, and in today's environment, no laptops, cell phones, iPods, or tablets. The wisdom of Noble Silence is that it closes all the escape routes and keeps your focus squarely on practice. After a while, even imagination gives up and you will find yourself dwelling in the present moment and experiencing the world in, perhaps, a way that you never have before. On a retreat you can have a taste of monastic life without having to make those commitments.

As mentioned earlier, a traditional retreat length is ten days. However, retreats come in many lengths, and they can be residential or nonresidential. For example, at the Cambridge Insight Meditation Center in Cambridge, Massachusetts, retreats are nonresidential and may be one or two days on a nine-to-five schedule. Other retreats can be three months long, and in one tradition there is a three-year-three-month-three days-long retreat! Better clear your calendar for that one!

Concentration provides the foundation for insight. And morality provides the foundation for everything. In addition to becoming intimate with your experience, meditation provides you the means to change your internal landscape from one characterized by dukkha to one characterized by freedom. Mindfulness is an integral component to every Buddhist tradition and is, in fact, the method Siddhartha Gotama used to become the Buddha.

AWAKE AT WORK

Being Fully Engaged

If you are like most people, you spend at least forty hours or more each week at your job. You also spend time commuting back and forth to that job. The time devoted to work is roughly half of your waking life. How do you want to spend this time? If you live your life waiting for the weekends and vacations to "really live," then you are spending most of your life waiting and not living. The Buddha's message provides you a way to be fully engaged with whatever you are doing and this means, most of the time, your job. Being awake at work is one of the more challenging places to be awake. There are petty tyrant bosses, mindless colleagues, and not much evidence of the Noble Eightfold Path in action. If you are not awake at work, work will be stressful.

Stress is one of the most pervasive and insidious problems facing the workplace today. It is estimated that stress costs American corporations $300 billion annually, or $7,500 per worker per year when lost hours due to absenteeism, reduced productivity, and workers' compensation benefits are considered.

If you approach your work life as a necessity and an obligation, you might neglect its "soul" elements. The poet, corporate consultant, and Zen practitioner David Whyte suggests that connecting with your soul at work is a responsibility, not a luxury. In his three books on work life, *The Heart Aroused: Poetry and the Preservation of the Soul in Corporate America; Crossing the Unknown Sea: Work as Pilgrimage of Identity*, and *The Three Marriages: Reimaging Self, Work, and Relationship*, he identifies work as a place of sacred visibility. It is the expression of the public, community-serving self. It is the reflection of core values of competence, effectiveness, and accomplishment. If you are disconnected, dissatisfied, or disgruntled with your work experience a significant portion of yourself may be compromised.

"Human beings must, in a sense, always, in order to create meaning, in order to create an ecology of belonging around them, must bring the central questions of their life into whatever they are doing most of the time."

—David Whyte

The workplace is the source of many conditioned reactions. Greed, hatred, and delusion are frequent visitors. Generosity, loving-kindness, and wisdom are perhaps less frequent. Today's workplace is also a place of great uncertainty, and each moment at work may be a reflection of impermanence. Mindfulness can help you to steel yourself against this uncertainty.

Work may be an unavoidable intrusion into life. For some, there is great joy in work. A *New York Times* article featuring mindfulness for physicians described one surgeon who said, "Time in the O.R. is not work; it's play." That's the Buddha at work!

INDEX

BUDDHISM 101